HEART SPEAKS UNTO HEART

HEART SPEAKS UNTO HEART

POPE BENEDICT XVI IN THE UK

THE COMPLETE ADDRESSES AND HOMILIES

DARTON · LONGMAN + TODD

First published in 2010 by
Darton, Longman and Todd Ltd
1 Spencer Court
140–142 Wandsworth High Street
London SW18 4JJ

ISBN 978-0-232-52841-1 (cased)
ISBN 978-0-232-52842-8 (paper)

A catalogue record for this book is available from the British Library

Phototypeset by Kerrypress Ltd, Luton, Bedfordshire
Printed and bound in Great Britain by CPI Antony Rowe, Chippenham

Contents

Introduction

As Archbishop Vincent Nichols said in his parting words, Pope Benedict's addresses and homilies during his visit to the United Kingdom in 2010 have made a rich contribution to our history and to the shaping of our future. They are collected here, so that they can be studied in full, together with addresses of welcome by Her Majesty The Queen, the Archbishop of Canterbury, Dr Rowan Williams, and the Chief Rabbi, Lord Sacks.

The theme Pope Benedict chose for his visit was *Cor ad cor loquitur* – "Heart speaks unto heart". These were the words Blessed John Henry Newman chose for his coat of arms when he became a Cardinal. The climax of the Pope's visit was the beatification of Newman in Birmingham on 19 September.

Openness of heart, obedience to conscience, faithfulness to the gospel whatever the cost, attentive and respectful listening, the importance of dialogue, conversation and friendship. These motifs appear again and again in Newman's writings and they mark all the Pope's addresses and homilies.

"Heart speaks unto heart." The Pope sought to start a national conversation about the role of faith in society.

Addressing political and civic leaders in the historic setting of Westminster Hall, he was generous in his praise of the British instinct for moderation and tolerance. But he argued that the freedoms of our pluralist and democratic society are underpinned by Christian foundations, and that they would be weakened if religion were to be marginalised or silenced.

He asked the leaders of other faith communities to join him in open and reciprocal dialogue. At Westminster Abbey, he commended the Venerable Bede for his faithfulness to the word of God and his creative openness to contemporary language and culture. Responding to the warm greeting of the Archbishop of Canterbury, he called all Christians into deeper prayer and dialogue, in a search for the truth undertaken side by side in friendship and love.

"Heart speaks unto heart." The Pope spent time with the elderly residents of a care home, and enjoyed an exuberant celebration of Catholic education with pupils and teachers. He asked for attention to be drawn to the world's poor. Surely, he said, they are no less important than the financial institutions that were rescued at vast public expense.

The Pope's most heartfelt moments were when he expressed his deep sorrow and shame at the suffering caused by the abuse of children by Catholic priests. He met survivors of abuse, and a group of those responsible for ensuring that the preventative measures now in place are effective and that any allegations of abuse are dealt with swiftly and justly in future.

"Heart speaks unto heart." At the deepest level, these words refer to the innate desire of the human heart for intimate communion with the Heart of God. "Even now", the Pope reminded the crowd listening quietly to his homily at the Vigil of Prayer and the Exposition of the Blessed Sacrament in Hyde Park, "God's heart is speaking to your heart."

Brendan Walsh

Thursday
16 September

Palace of Holyrood House, Edinburgh

Address of Welcome by Her Majesty The Queen

Pope Benedict XVI arrived in Scotland on the morning of Thursday 16 September for the first State visit of a Pope to Great Britain. He was greeted at Edinburgh International Airport by the Duke of Edinburgh, former Archbishop of Westminster Cardinal Cormac Murphy-O'Connor and Cardinal Keith O'Brien, head of the Catholic Church in Scotland. At a State Reception in the grounds of the Palace of Holyrood House, the official residence of Her Majesty Queen Elizabeth II, The Queen and Pope Benedict exchanged the following greetings.

Your Holiness,

I am delighted to welcome you to the United Kingdom, and particularly to Scotland, on your first visit as Pope. I recall with great pleasure the memorable pastoral visit of the late Pope John Paul II to this country in 1982. I also have vivid memories of my four visits to the Vatican, and of meeting some of your predecessors on other occasions. I am most grateful to them for receiving, over the years, a number of members of my family with such warm hospitality.

Much has changed in the world during the nearly thirty years since Pope John Paul's visit. In this country, we deeply appreciate the involvement of the Holy See in the dramatic improvement in the situation in Northern Ireland. Elsewhere the fall of totalitarian regimes across central and Eastern Europe has allowed greater freedom for hundreds of millions of people. The Holy See continues to have an important role in international issues, in support of peace and development and in addressing common problems like poverty and climate change.

Your Holiness, your presence here today reminds us of our common Christian heritage, and of the Christian contribution to the encouragement of world peace, and to the economic and social development of the less prosperous countries of the world. We are all aware of the special contribution of the Roman Catholic Church particularly in its ministry to the poorest and most deprived members of society, its care for the homeless and for the education provided by its extensive network of schools.

Religion has always been a crucial element in national identity and historical self-consciousness. This has made the relationship between the different faiths a fundamental factor in the necessary cooperation within and between nation states. It is, therefore, vital to encourage a greater mutual, and respectful understanding. We know from experience that through committed dialogue, old suspicions can be transcended and a greater mutual trust established.

I know that reconciliation was a central theme in the life of Cardinal John Henry Newman, for whom you will be holding a Mass of Beatification on Sunday. A man who struggled with doubt and uncertainty, his contribution to the understanding of Christianity continues to influence many. I am pleased that your visit will also provide an opportunity to deepen the relationship between the Roman Catholic Church and the established Church of England and the Church of Scotland.

Your Holiness, in recent times you have said that "religions can never become vehicles of hatred, that never by invoking the name of God can evil and violence be justified". Today, in this country, we stand united in that conviction. We hold that freedom to worship is at the core of our tolerant and democratic society.

On behalf of the people of the United Kingdom I wish you a most fruitful and memorable visit.

Palace of Holyrood House, Edinburgh

Address on Arrival in the United Kingdom

Your Majesty,

Thank you for your gracious invitation to make an official visit to the United Kingdom and for your warm words of greeting on behalf of the British people. In thanking Your Majesty, allow me to extend my own greetings to all the people of the United Kingdom and to hold out a hand of friendship to each one.

It is a great pleasure for me to start my journey by saluting the members of the Royal Family, thanking in particular His Royal Highness the Duke of Edinburgh for his kind welcome to me at Edinburgh Airport. I express my gratitude to Your Majesty's present and previous Governments and to all those who worked with them to make this occasion possible, including Lord Patten and former Secretary of State Murphy. I would also like to acknowledge with deep appreciation the work of the All-Party Parliamentary Group on the Holy See, which has contributed greatly to strengthening the friendly relations existing between the Holy See and the United Kingdom.

As I begin my visit to the United Kingdom in Scotland's historic capital city, I greet in a special way First Minister Salmond and the representatives of the Scottish Parliament. Just like the Welsh and Northern Ireland Assemblies, may the Scottish Parliament grow to be an expression of the fine traditions and distinct culture of the Scots and strive to serve their best interests in a spirit of solidarity and concern for the common good.

The name of Holyroodhouse, Your Majesty's official residence in Scotland, recalls the "Holy Cross" and points to the deep Christian roots that are still present in every layer of British life. The monarchs of England

and Scotland have been Christians from very early times and include outstanding saints like Edward the Confessor and Margaret of Scotland. As you know, many of them consciously exercised their sovereign duty in the light of the Gospel, and in this way shaped the nation for good at the deepest level. As a result, the Christian message has been an integral part of the language, thought and culture of the peoples of these islands for more than a thousand years. Your forefathers' respect for truth and justice, for mercy and charity come to you from a faith that remains a mighty force for good in your kingdom, to the great benefit of Christians and non-Christians alike.

We find many examples of this force for good throughout Britain's long history. Even in comparatively recent times, due to figures like William Wilberforce and David Livingstone, Britain intervened directly to stop the international slave trade. Inspired by faith, women like Florence Nightingale served the poor and the sick and set new standards in healthcare that were subsequently copied everywhere. John Henry Newman, whose beatification I will celebrate shortly, was one of many British Christians of his age whose goodness, eloquence and action were a credit to their countrymen and women. These, and many people like them, were inspired by a deep faith born and nurtured in these islands.

Even in our own lifetime, we can recall how Britain and her leaders stood against a Nazi tyranny that wished to eradicate God from society and denied our common humanity to many, especially the Jews, who were thought unfit to live. I also recall the regime's attitude to Christian pastors and religious who spoke the truth in love, opposed the Nazis and paid for that opposition with their lives. As we reflect on the sobering lessons of the atheist extremism of the twentieth century, let us never forget how the exclusion of God, religion and virtue from public life leads ultimately to a truncated vision of man and of society and thus to a "reductive vision of the person and his destiny" (*Caritas in Veritate*, 29).

Sixty-five years ago, Britain played an essential role in forging the post-war international consensus which favoured the establishment of the United Nations and ushered in a hitherto unknown period of peace and prosperity in Europe. In more recent years, the international community has followed closely events in Northern Ireland which have led to the signing of the Good Friday Agreement and the devolution of powers to the Northern Ireland Assembly. Your Majesty's Government and the Government of Ireland, together with the political, religious and civil leaders of Northern Ireland, have helped give birth to a peaceful resolution of the conflict there. I encourage everyone involved to continue to walk courageously together on the path marked out for them towards a just and lasting peace.

Looking abroad, the United Kingdom remains a key figure politically and economically on the international stage. Your Government and people are the shapers of ideas that still have an impact far beyond the British Isles. This places upon them a particular duty to act wisely for the common good. Similarly, because their opinions reach such a wide audience, the British media have a graver responsibility than most and a greater opportunity to promote the peace of nations, the integral development of peoples and the spread of authentic human rights. May all Britons continue to live by the values of honesty, respect and fair-mindedness that have won them the esteem and admiration of many.

Today, the United Kingdom strives to be a modern and multicultural society. In this challenging enterprise, may it always maintain its respect for those traditional values and cultural expressions that more aggressive forms of secularism no longer value or even tolerate. Let it not obscure the Christian foundation that underpins its freedoms; and may that patrimony, which has always served the nation well, constantly inform the example your Government and people set before the two billion members of the Commonwealth and the great family of English-speaking nations throughout the world.

May God bless Your Majesty and all the people of your realm. Thank you.

Bellahouston Park, Glasgow

Homily at Bellahouston Park

Pope Benedict travelled in the popemobile from Holyrood Palace to Cardinal Keith O'Brien's official residence. 125,000 people lined the route along Regent Road, Waterloo Place and Princes Street for a St Ninian's Day parade to welcome the Pope to Scotland. After a private lunch at Archbishop's House, Pope Benedict was driven to Glasgow, where he presided in the evening at the celebration of Mass for a crowd of 65,000 people in Bellahouston Park, and delivered the following homily. After Mass, he flew from Glasgow airport to London Heathrow. He stayed the night at the home of the Apostolic Nuncio in Wimbledon, west London.

Dear Brothers and Sisters in Christ,

"The Kingdom of God is very near to you!" (Lk 10:9). With these words of the Gospel we have just heard, I greet all of you with great affection in the Lord. Truly the Lord's Kingdom is already in our midst! At this Eucharistic celebration in which the Church in Scotland gathers around the altar in union with the Successor of Peter, let us reaffirm our faith in Christ's word and our hope – a hope which never disappoints – in his promises! I warmly greet Cardinal O'Brien and the Scottish Bishops; I thank in particular Archbishop Conti for his kind words of welcome on your behalf;

and I express my deep gratitude for the work that the British and Scottish Governments and the Glasgow city fathers have done to make this occasion possible.

Today's Gospel reminds us that Christ continues to send his disciples into the world in order to proclaim the coming of his Kingdom and to bring his peace into the world, beginning house by house, family by family, town by town. I have come as a herald of that peace to you, the spiritual children of Saint Andrew and to confirm you in the faith of Peter (cf.Lk 22:32). It is with some emotion that I address you, not far from the spot where my beloved predecessor Pope John Paul II celebrated Mass nearly thirty years ago with you and was welcomed by the largest crowd ever gathered in Scottish history.

Much has happened in Scotland and in the Church in this country since that historic visit. I note with great satisfaction how Pope John Paul's call to you to walk hand in hand with your fellow Christians has led to greater trust and friendship with the members of the Church of Scotland, the Scottish Episcopal Church and others. Let me encourage you to continue to pray and work with them in building a brighter future for Scotland based upon our common Christian heritage. In today's first reading we heard Saint Paul appeal to the Romans to acknowledge that, as members of Christ's body, we belong to each other (cf. Rom 12:5) and to live in respect and mutual love. In that spirit I greet the ecumenical representatives who honour us by their presence. This year marks the 450th anniversary of the Reformation Parliament, but also the 100th anniversary of the World Missionary Conference in Edinburgh, which is widely acknowledged to mark the birth of the modern ecumenical movement. Let us give thanks to God for the promise which ecumenical understanding and cooperation represents for a united witness to the saving truth of God's word in today's rapidly changing society.

Among the differing gifts which Saint Paul lists for the building up of the Church is that of teaching (cf. Rom 12:7). The preaching of the Gospel has always been accompanied by concern for the word: the inspired word of God and the culture in which that word takes root and flourishes. Here in Scotland, I think of the three medieval universities founded here by the popes, including that of Saint Andrews which is beginning to mark the 600th anniversary of its foundation. In the last 30 years and with the assistance of civil authorities, Scottish Catholic schools have taken up the challenge of providing an integral education to greater numbers of students, and this has helped young people not only along the path of spiritual and human growth, but also in entering the professions and public life. This is a sign of great hope for the Church, and I encourage the Catholic professionals, politicians and teachers of Scotland never to lose sight of their calling to use their talents and experience in the service of the faith, engaging contemporary Scottish culture at every level.

The evangelization of culture is all the more important in our times, when a "dictatorship of relativism" threatens to obscure the unchanging truth about man's nature, his destiny and his ultimate good. There are some who now seek to exclude religious belief from public discourse, to privatize it or even to paint it as a threat to equality and liberty. Yet religion is in fact a guarantee of authentic liberty and respect, leading us to look upon every person as a brother or sister. For this reason I appeal in particular to you, the lay faithful, in accordance with your baptismal calling and mission, not only to be examples of faith in public, but also to put the case for the promotion of faith's wisdom and vision in the public forum. Society today needs clear voices which propose our right to live, not in a jungle of self-destructive and arbitrary freedoms, but in a society which works for the true welfare of its citizens and offers them guidance and protection in the face of their weakness and fragility. Do not be afraid to take up this service to your brothers and sisters, and to the future of your beloved nation.

Saint Ninian, whose feast we celebrate today, was himself unafraid to be a lone voice. In the footsteps of the disciples whom our Lord sent forth before him, Ninian was one of the very first Catholic missionaries to bring his fellow Britons the good news of Jesus Christ.

His mission church in Galloway became a centre for the first evangelization of this country. That work was later taken up by Saint Mungo, Glasgow's own patron, and by other saints, the greatest of who must include Saint Columba and Saint Margaret. Inspired by them, many men and women have laboured over many centuries to hand down the faith to you. Strive to be worthy of this great tradition! Let the exhortation of Saint Paul in the first reading be your constant inspiration: "Do not lag in zeal, be ardent in spirit, serve the Lord. Rejoice in hope, be patient in suffering and persevere in prayer" (cf. Rom 12:11–12).

I would now like to address a special word to the bishops of Scotland. Dear brothers, let me encourage you in your pastoral leadership of the Catholics of Scotland. As you know, one of your first pastoral duties is to your priests (cf. *Presbyterorum Ordinis*, 7) and to their sanctification. As they are *alter Christus* to the Catholic community, so you are to them. Live to the full the charity that flows from Christ, in your brotherly ministry towards your priests, collaborating with them all, and in particular with those who have little contact with their fellow priests. Pray with them for vocations, that the Lord of the harvest will send labourers to his harvest (cf. Lk 10:2). Just as the Eucharist makes the Church, so the priesthood is central to the life of the Church. Engage yourselves personally in forming your priests as a body of men who inspire others to dedicate themselves completely to the service of Almighty God. Have a care also for your deacons, whose ministry of service is associated in a particular way with that of the order of bishops. Be a father and a guide in holiness for them, encouraging them to grow in knowledge and wisdom in carrying out the mission of herald to which they have been called.

Dear priests of Scotland, you are called to holiness and to serve God's people by modelling your lives on the mystery of the Lord's cross. Preach the Gospel with a pure heart and a clear conscience. Dedicate yourselves to God alone and you will become shining examples to young men of a holy, simple and joyful life: they, in their turn, will surely wish to join you in your single-minded service of God's people. May the example of Saint John Ogilvie, dedicated, selfless and brave, inspire all of you. Similarly, let me encourage you, the monks, nuns and religious of Scotland to be a light on a hilltop, living an authentic Christian life of prayer and action that witnesses in a luminous way to the power of the Gospel.

Finally, I would like to say a word to you, my dear young Catholics of Scotland. I urge you to lead lives worthy of our Lord (cf. Eph 4:1) and of yourselves. There are many temptations placed before you every day – drugs, money, sex, pornography, alcohol – which the world tells you will bring you happiness, yet these things are destructive and divisive. There is only one thing which lasts: the love of Jesus Christ personally for each one of you. Search for him, know him and love him, and he will set you free from slavery to the glittering but superficial existence frequently proposed by today's society. Put aside what is worthless and learn of your own dignity as children of God. In today's Gospel, Jesus asks us to pray for vocations: I pray that many of you will know and love Jesus Christ and, through that encounter, will dedicate yourselves completely to God, especially those of you who are called to the priesthood and religious life. This is the challenge the Lord gives to you today: the Church now belongs to you!

Dear friends, I express once more my joy at celebrating this Mass with you. I am happy to assure you of my prayers in the ancient language of your country: *Sìth agus beannachd Dhe dhuibh uile; Dia bhi timcheall oirbh; agus gum beannaicheadh Dia Alba.* God's peace and blessing to you all; God surround you; and may God bless the people of Scotland!

Friday
17 September

Chapel of St Mary's University College, Strawberry Hill

Address to Teachers and Religious

After the private celebration of Mass in the chapel of the Apostolic Nunciature, Pope Benedict visited St Mary's University College, Strawberry Hill, in south-west London, where he gave three addresses. After a service of prayer in the college chapel he spoke as follows to representatives of religious congregations and others in the teaching profession.

Your Excellency the Secretary of State for Education, Bishop Stack, Dr Naylor, Reverend Fathers, Brothers and Sisters in Christ,

I am pleased to have this opportunity to pay tribute to the outstanding contribution made by religious men and women in this land to the noble task of education. I thank the young people for their fine singing, and I thank Sister Teresa for her words. To her and to all the dedicated men and women who devote their lives to teaching the young, I want to express sentiments of deep appreciation. You form new generations not only in knowledge of the faith, but in every aspect of what it means to live as mature and responsible citizens in today's world.

As you know, the task of a teacher is not simply to impart information or to provide training in skills intended to deliver some economic benefit to society; education is not and must never be considered as purely utilitarian. It is about forming the human person, equipping him or her to live life to the full – in short it is about imparting wisdom. And true wisdom is inseparable from knowledge of the Creator, for "both we and our words are in his hand, as are all understanding and skill in crafts" (Wis 7:16).

This transcendent dimension of study and teaching was clearly grasped by the monks who contributed so much to the evangelization of these islands. I am thinking of the Benedictines who accompanied Saint Augustine on his mission to England, of the disciples of Saint Columba who spread the faith across Scotland and Northern England, of Saint David and his companions in Wales. Since the search for God, which lies at the heart of the monastic vocation, requires active engagement with the means by which he makes himself known – his creation and his revealed word – it was only natural that the monastery should have a library and a school (cf. Address to representatives from the world of culture at the "Collège des Bernardins" in Paris, 12 September 2008). It was the monks' dedication to learning as the path on which to encounter the Incarnate Word of God that was to lay the foundations of our Western culture and civilization.

Looking around me today, I see many apostolic religious whose charism includes the education of the young. This gives me an opportunity to give thanks to God for the life and work of the Venerable Mary Ward, a native of this land whose pioneering vision of apostolic religious life for women has borne so much fruit. I myself as a young boy was taught by the "English Ladies" and I owe them a deep debt of gratitude. Many of you belong to teaching orders that have carried the light of the Gospel to far-off lands as part of the Church's great missionary work, and for this too I give thanks and praise to God. Often you laid the foundations of educational provision long before the State assumed a responsibility for this vital service to the individual and to society. As the relative roles of Church and State in the field of education continue to evolve, never forget that religious have a unique contribution to offer to this apostolate, above all through lives consecrated to God and through faithful, loving witness to Christ, the supreme Teacher.

Indeed, the presence of religious in Catholic schools is a powerful reminder of the much-discussed Catholic ethos that needs to inform every aspect of school life. This extends far beyond the self-evident requirement that the content of the teaching should always be in conformity with Church doctrine. It means that the life of faith needs to be the driving force behind every activity in the school, so that the Church's mission may be served effectively, and the young people may discover the joy of entering into Christ's "being for others" (*Spe Salvi*, 28).

Before I conclude, I wish to add a particular word of appreciation for those whose task it is to ensure that our schools provide a safe environment for children and young people. Our responsibility towards those entrusted to us for their Christian formation demands nothing less. Indeed, the life of faith can only be effectively nurtured when the prevailing atmosphere is one of respectful and affectionate trust. I pray that this may continue to be a hallmark of the Catholic schools in this country.

With these sentiments, dear Brothers and Sisters, I invite you now to stand and pray.

Sports Arena of St Mary's University College

Address to school children and students

From the chapel, Pope Benedict went to the sports arena for a Celebration of Catholic Education with 4,000 young children and teachers. The event was connected over the web to schools in the United Kingdom and overseas, and was described as possibly the largest school assembly in history. The Pope spoke as follows.

Dear Brothers and Sisters in Christ, Dear young friends,

First of all, I want to say how glad I am to be here with you today. I greet you most warmly, those who have come to Saint Mary's University from Catholic schools and colleges across the United Kingdom, and all who are watching on television and via the internet. I thank Bishop McMahon for his gracious welcome, I thank the choir and the band for the lovely music which began our celebration, and I thank Miss Bellot for her kind words on behalf of all the young people present. In view of London's forthcoming Olympic Games, it has been a pleasure to inaugurate this Sports Foundation, named in honour of Pope John Paul II, and I pray that all who come here will give glory to God through their sporting activities, as well as bringing enjoyment to themselves and to others.

It is not often that a Pope, or indeed anyone else, has the opportunity to speak to the students of all the Catholic schools of England, Wales and Scotland at the same time. And since I have the chance now, there is something I very much want to say to you. I hope that among those of you listening to me today there are some of the future saints of the twenty-first century. What God wants most of all for each one of you is that you should become holy. He loves you much more than you could ever begin to imagine, and he wants the very best for you. And by far the best thing for you is to grow in holiness.

Perhaps some of you have never thought about this before. Perhaps some of you think being a saint is not for you. Let me explain what I mean. When we are young, we can usually think of people that we look up to, people we admire, people we want to be like. It could be someone we meet in our daily lives that we hold in great esteem. Or it could be someone famous. We live in a celebrity culture, and young people are often encouraged to model themselves on figures from the world of sport or entertainment. My question for you is this: what are the qualities you see in others that you would most like to have yourselves? What kind of person would you really like to be?

When I invite you to become saints, I am asking you not to be content with second best. I am asking you not to pursue one limited goal and ignore all the others. Having money makes it possible to be generous and to do good in the world, but on its own, it is not enough to make us happy. Being highly skilled in some activity or profession is good, but it will not satisfy us unless we aim for something greater still. It might make us famous, but it will not make us happy. Happiness is something we all want, but one of the great tragedies in this world is that so many people never find it, because they look for it in the wrong places. The key to it is very simple – true happiness is to be found in God. We need to have the courage to place our deepest hopes in God alone, not in money, in a career, in worldly success, or in our relationships with others, but in God. Only he can satisfy the deepest needs of our hearts.

Not only does God love us with a depth and an intensity that we can scarcely begin to comprehend, but he invites us to respond to that love. You all know what it is like when you meet someone interesting and attractive, and you want to be that person's friend. You always hope they will find you interesting and attractive, and want to be your friend. God wants your friendship. And once you enter into friendship with God, everything in your life begins to change. As you come to know him better, you find you want to reflect something of his infinite goodness in your own life. You are attracted to the practice of virtue. You begin to see greed and selfishness and all the other sins for what they really are, destructive and dangerous tendencies that cause deep suffering and do great damage, and you want to avoid falling into that trap yourselves. You begin to feel compassion for people in difficulties and you are eager to do something to help them. You want to come to the aid of the poor and the hungry, you want to comfort the sorrowful, you want to be kind and generous. And once these things begin to matter to you, you are well on the way to becoming saints.

In your Catholic schools, there is always a bigger picture over and above the individual subjects you study, the different skills you learn. All the work you do is placed in the context of growing in friendship with God, and all that flows from that friendship. So you learn not just to be good students, but good citizens, good people. As you move higher up the school, you have to make choices regarding the subjects you study, you begin to specialize with a view to what you are going to do later on in life. That is right and proper. But always remember that every subject you study is part of a bigger picture. Never allow yourselves to become narrow. The world needs good scientists, but a scientific outlook becomes dangerously narrow if it ignores the religious or ethical dimension of life, just as religion becomes narrow if it rejects the legitimate contribution of science to our understanding of the world. We need good historians and philosophers and economists, but if the account they give of human life within their particular field is too narrowly focused, they can lead us seriously astray.

A good school provides a rounded education for the whole person. And a good Catholic school, over and above this, should help all its students to become saints. I know that there are many non-Catholics studying in the Catholic schools in Great Britain, and I wish to include all of you in my words today. I pray that you too will feel encouraged to practise virtue and to grow in knowledge and friendship with God alongside your Catholic classmates. You are a reminder to them of the bigger picture that exists outside the school, and indeed, it is only right that respect and friendship for members of other religious traditions should be among the virtues learned in a Catholic school. I hope too that you will want to share with everyone you meet the values and insights you have learned through the Christian education you have received.

Dear friends, I thank you for your attention, I promise to pray for you, and I ask you to pray for me. I hope to see many of you next August, at the World Youth Day in Madrid. In the meantime, may God bless you all!

Waldegrave Drawing Room, St Mary's University College

The Chief Rabbi's Address to Pope Benedict

The Pope then met with clerical and lay representatives of other religions in the historic Drawing Room of St Mary's College. He was welcomed by the Chief Rabbi, Lord Sacks, who spoke as follows:

We welcome you, leader of a great faith, to this gathering of many faiths, in a land where once battles were fought in the name of faith, and where now we share friendship across faiths.

That is a climate change worth celebrating. And we recognise the immense role the Vatican played and continues to play in bringing it about. It was *Nostra Aetate*, forty-five years ago, that brought about the single greatest transformation in interfaith relations in recent history, and we recognise your visit here today as a new chapter in that story, and a vital one.

The secularization of Europe that began in the seventeenth century did not happen because people lost faith in God. Newton and Descartes, heroes of the Enlightenment, believed in God very much indeed. What led to secularization was that people lost faith in the ability of people of faith to live peaceably together. And we must never go down that road again. We remember the fine words of John Henry Cardinal Newman, "We should ever conduct ourselves towards our enemy as if he were one day to be our friend", as well as your own words, in *Caritas in Veritate*, that "the development of peoples depends ... on a recognition that the human race is a single family, working together in true communion, not simply a group of subjects who happen to live side by side".

We celebrate both our commonalities and differences, because if we had nothing in common we could not communicate, and if we had everything in common, we would have nothing to say. You have spoken of the Catholic Church as a creative minority. And perhaps that is what we should all aspire to be, creative minorities, inspiring one another, and bringing our different gifts to the common good.

Britain has been so enriched by its minorities, by every group represented here today and the intricate harmonies of our several voices. And one of our commonalities is that we surely all believe that faith has a major role in strengthening civil society.

In the face of a deeply individualistic culture, we offer community. Against consumerism, we talk about the things that have value but not a price. Against cynicism we dare to admire and respect. In the face of fragmenting families, we believe in consecrating relationships. We believe in marriage as a commitment, parenthood as a responsibility, and the poetry of everyday life when it is etched, in homes and schools, with the charisma of holiness and grace.

In our communities we value people not for what they earn or what they buy or how they vote but for what they are, every one of them a fragment of the Divine presence. We hold life holy. And each of us is lifted by the knowledge that we are part of something greater than all of us, that created us in forgiveness and love, and asks us to create in forgiveness and love. Each of us in our own way is a guardian of values that are in danger of being lost, in our short-attention-span, hyperactive, information-saturated, wisdom-starved age. And though our faiths are profoundly different, yet we recognize in one another the presence of faith itself, that habit of the heart that listens to the music beneath the noise, and knows that God is the point at which soul touches soul and is enlarged by the presence of otherness.

You have honoured us with your presence, and we honour you. May you continue to lead with wisdom and generosity of spirit, and may all our efforts combine to become a blessing to humanity and to God.

Waldegrave Drawing Room, St Mary's University College

Speech to Religious Leaders

The Pope then addressed religious leaders in the historic Drawing Room of St Mary's College.

Distinguished guests, dear friends,

I am very pleased to have this opportunity to meet you, the representatives of the various religious communities in Great Britain. I greet both the ministers of religion present and those of you who are active in politics, business and industry. I am grateful to Dr Azzam and to Chief Rabbi, Lord Sacks, for the greetings which they have expressed on your behalf. As I salute you, let me also wish the Jewish community in Britain and throughout the world a happy and holy celebration of Yom Kippur.

I would like to begin my remarks by expressing the Catholic Church's appreciation for the important witness that all of you bear as spiritual men and women living at a time when religious convictions are not always understood or appreciated. The presence of committed believers in various fields of social and economic life speaks eloquently of the fact that the spiritual dimension of our lives is fundamental to our identity as human beings, that man, in other words, does not live by bread alone (cf. Deut 8:3). As followers of different religious traditions working together for the good of the community at large, we attach great importance to this "side by side" dimension of our cooperation, which complements the "face to face" aspect of our continuing dialogue.

On the spiritual level, all of us, in our different ways, are personally engaged in a journey that grants an answer to the most important question of all – the question concerning the ultimate meaning of our human existence. The quest for the sacred is the search for the one thing necessary, which alone satisfies the longings of the human heart. In the fifth century, Saint Augustine described that search in these terms: "Lord, you have created us for yourself and our hearts are restless until they rest in you" (*Confessions*, Book I, 1). As we embark on this adventure we come to realize more and more that the initiative lies not with us, but with the Lord: it is not so much we who are seeking him, but rather he who is seeking us, indeed it was he who placed that longing for him deep within our hearts.

Your presence and witness in the world points towards the fundamental importance for human life of this spiritual quest in which we are engaged. Within their own spheres of competence, the human and natural sciences provide us with an invaluable understanding of aspects of our existence and they deepen our grasp of the workings of the physical universe, which can then be harnessed in order to bring great benefit to the human family. Yet these disciplines do not and cannot answer the fundamental question, because they operate on another level altogether. They cannot satisfy the deepest longings of the human heart, they cannot fully explain to us our origin and our destiny, why and for what purpose we exist, nor indeed can they provide us with an exhaustive answer to the question, "Why is there something rather than nothing?"

The quest for the sacred does not devalue other fields of human enquiry. On the contrary, it places them in a context which magnifies their importance, as ways of responsibly exercising our stewardship over creation. In the Bible, we read that, after the work of creation was completed, God blessed our first parents and said to them, "Be fruitful and multiply, and fill the earth and subdue it" (Gen 1:28). He entrusted us with the task of exploring and harnessing the mysteries of nature in order to serve a higher good. What is that higher good? In the Christian faith, it is expressed as love for God and love for our neighbour. And so we engage with the world wholeheartedly and enthusiastically, but always with a view to serving that higher good, lest we disfigure the beauty of creation by exploiting it for selfish purposes.

So it is that genuine religious belief points us beyond present utility towards the transcendent. It reminds us of the possibility and the imperative of moral conversion, of the duty to live peaceably with our neighbour, of the importance of living a life of integrity. Properly understood, it brings enlightenment, it purifies our hearts and it inspires noble and generous action, to the benefit of the entire human family. It motivates us to cultivate the practice of virtue and to reach out towards one another in love, with the greatest respect for religious traditions different from our own.

Ever since the Second Vatican Council, the Catholic Church has placed special emphasis on the importance of dialogue and cooperation with the followers of other religions. In order to be fruitful, this requires reciprocity on the part of all partners in dialogue and the followers of other religions. I am thinking in particular of situations in some parts of the world, where cooperation and dialogue between religions calls for mutual respect, the freedom to practise one's religion and to engage in acts of public worship, and the freedom to follow one's conscience without suffering ostracism or persecution, even after conversion from one religion to another. Once such a respect and openness has been established, peoples of all religions will work together effectively for peace and mutual understanding, and so give a convincing witness before the world.

This kind of dialogue needs to take place on a number of different levels, and should not be limited to formal discussions. The dialogue of life involves simply living alongside one another and learning from one another in such a way as to grow in mutual knowledge and respect. The dialogue of action brings us together in concrete forms of collaboration, as we apply our religious insights to the task of promoting integral human development, working for peace, justice and the stewardship of creation. Such a dialogue may include exploring together how to defend human life at every stage and how to ensure the non-exclusion of the religious dimension of individuals and communities in the life of society. Then at the level of formal conversations, there is a need not only for theological exchange, but also sharing our spiritual riches, speaking of our experience of prayer and contemplation, and expressing to one another the joy of our encounter with divine love. In this context I am pleased to note the many positive initiatives undertaken in this country to promote such dialogue at a variety of levels. As the Catholic Bishops of England and Wales noted in their recent document *Meeting God in Friend and Stranger*, the effort to reach out in friendship to followers of other religions is becoming a familiar part of the mission of the local Church (n. 228), a characteristic feature of the religious landscape in this country.

My dear friends, as I conclude my remarks, let me assure you that the Catholic Church follows the path of engagement and dialogue out of a genuine sense of respect for you and your beliefs. Catholics, both in Britain and throughout the world, will continue to work to build bridges of friendship to other religions, to heal past wrongs and to foster trust between individuals and communities. Let me reiterate my thanks for your welcome and my gratitude for this opportunity to offer you my encouragement for your dialogue with your Christian sisters and brothers. Upon all of you I invoke abundant divine blessings! Thank you very much.

Lambeth Palace

Archbishop of Canterbury's Address to Pope Benedict

On Friday afternoon, Pope Benedict made a fraternal visit to Dr Rowan Williams, the Archbishop of Canterbury, at Lambeth Palace, where they both addressed the Anglican and Roman Catholic Diocesan Bishops of England, Scotland and Wales in the Great Hall of the Archbishop's Library.

Your Holiness, brother bishops, brothers and sisters in Christ:

It is a particular pleasure that on this historic occasion we are able to come together as bishops of the Roman Catholic and Anglican churches in this country to greet you, Your Holiness, during a visit which we all hope will be of significance both to the Church of Christ and to British society. Your consistent and penetrating analysis of the state of European society in general has been a major contribution to public debate on the relations between Church and culture, and we gratefully acknowledge our debt in this respect.

Our task as bishops is to preach the Gospel and shepherd the flock of Christ; and this includes the responsibility not only to feed but also to protect it from harm. Today, this involves a readiness to respond to the various trends in our cultural environment that seek to present Christian faith as both an obstacle to human freedom and a scandal to human intellect. We need to be clear that the Gospel of the new creation in Jesus Christ is the door through which we enter into true liberty and true understanding: we are made free to be human as God intends us to be human; we are given the illumination that helps us see one another and all created things in the light of divine love and intelligence. As you said in your Inaugural Mass in 2005, recalling your predecessor's first words as pope, Christ takes away nothing "that pertains to human freedom or dignity or to the building of a just society ... If we let Christ into our lives we lose absolutely nothing of what makes life free, beautiful and great. Only in his friendship is the great potential of human existence revealed" (*Inaugural Homily*, Rome, 24 April 2005).

Our presence together as British bishops here today is a sign of the way in which, in this country, we see our task as one and indivisible. The International Anglican-Roman Catholic Commission on Unity and Mission has set before us all the vital importance of our common calling as bishops to be agents of mission. Our fervent prayer is that this visit will give us fresh energy and vision for working together in this context in the name of what a great Roman Catholic thinker of the last century called "true humanism" – a passionate commitment to the dignity of all human beings, from the beginning to the end of life, and to a resistance to every tyranny that threatens to stifle or deny the place of the transcendent in human affairs.

We do not as churches seek political power or control, or the dominance of Christian faith in the public sphere; but the opportunity to testify, to argue, sometimes to protest, sometimes to affirm – to play our part in the public debates of our societies. And we shall, of course, be effective not when we have mustered enough political leverage to get our way but when we have persuaded our neighbours that the life of faith is a life well lived and joyfully lived.

In other words, we shall be effective defenders or proclaimers of our faith when we can show what a holy life looks like, a life in which the joy of God is transparently present. And this means that our ministry together as bishops across the still-surviving boundaries of our confessions is not only a search for how we best act together in the public arena; it is a quest together for holiness and transparency to God, a search for ways in which we may help each other to grow in the life of the Holy Spirit. As you have said, Your Holiness, "a joint fundamental testimony of faith ought to be given before a world which is torn by doubts and shaken by fears" (*Luther and the Unity of the Churches*, 1983).

In 1845, when John Henry Newman finally decided that he must follow his conscience and seek his future in serving God in communion with the See of Rome, one of his most intimate Anglican friends and allies, the priest Edward Bouverie Pusey, whose memory the Church of England marked in its liturgical calendar yesterday, wrote a moving meditation on this "parting of friends" in which he said of the separation between Anglicans and Roman Catholics: "it is what is unholy on both sides that keeps us apart".

That should not surprise us: holiness is at its simplest fellowship with Christ; and when that fellowship with Christ is brought to maturity, so is our fellowship with one another. As bishops, we are servants of the unity of Christ's people, Christ's one Body. And, meeting as we do as bishops of separated church communities, we must all feel that each of our own ministries is made less by the fact of our dividedness, a very real but imperfect communion. Perhaps we shall not quickly overcome the remaining obstacles to full, restored communion; but no obstacles stand in the way of our seeking, as a matter of joyful obedience to the Lord, more ways in which to build up one another in holiness by prayer and public celebration together, by closer friendship, and by growing together both in the challenging work of service for all whom Christ loves, and mission to all God has made.

May this historic visit be for all of us a special time of grace and of growth in our shared calling, as you, Your Holiness, bring us the word of the Gospel afresh.

Lambeth Palace

Pope Benedict's Address to the Archbishop of Canterbury

Your Grace,

It is a pleasure for me to be able to return the courtesy of the visits you have made to me in Rome by a fraternal visit to you here in your official residence. I thank you for your invitation and for the hospitality that you have so generously provided. I greet too the Anglican Bishops gathered here from different parts of the United Kingdom, my brother Bishops from the Catholic Dioceses of England, Wales and Scotland, and the ecumenical advisers who are present.

You have spoken, Your Grace, of the historic meeting that took place, almost thirty years ago, between two of our predecessors – Pope John Paul the Second and Archbishop Robert Runcie – in Canterbury Cathedral. There, in the very place where Saint Thomas of Canterbury bore witness to Christ by the shedding of his blood, they prayed together for the gift of unity among the followers of Christ. We continue today to pray for that gift, knowing that the unity Christ willed for his disciples will only come about in answer to prayer, through the action of the Holy Spirit, who ceaselessly renews the Church and guides her into the fullness of truth.

It is not my intention today to speak of the difficulties that the ecumenical path has encountered and continues to encounter. Those difficulties are well known to everyone here. Rather, I wish to join you in giving thanks for the deep friendship that has grown between us and for the remarkable progress that has been made in so many areas of dialogue during the forty years that have elapsed since the Anglican-Roman Catholic International Commission began its work. Let us entrust the fruits of that work to the Lord of the harvest, confident that he will bless our friendship with further significant growth.

The context in which dialogue takes place between the Anglican Communion and the Catholic Church has evolved in dramatic ways since the private meeting between Pope John XXIII and Archbishop Geoffrey Fisher in 1960. On the one hand, the surrounding culture is growing ever more distant from its Christian roots, despite a deep and widespread hunger for spiritual nourishment. On the other hand, the increasingly multicultural dimension of society, particularly marked in this country, brings with it the opportunity to encounter other religions. For us Christians this opens up the possibility of exploring, together with members of other religious traditions, ways of bearing witness to the transcendent dimension of the human person and the universal call to holiness, leading to the practice of virtue in our personal and social lives. Ecumenical cooperation in this task remains essential, and will surely bear fruit in promoting peace and harmony in a world that so often seems at risk of fragmentation.

At the same time, we Christians must never hesitate to proclaim our faith in the uniqueness of the salvation won for us by Christ, and to explore together a deeper understanding of the means he has placed at our disposal for attaining that salvation. God "wants all to be saved, and to come to the knowledge of the truth" (1 Tim 2:4), and that truth is nothing other than Jesus Christ, eternal Son of the Father, who has reconciled all things in himself by the power of his Cross. In fidelity to the Lord's will, as expressed in that passage from Saint Paul's First Letter to Timothy, we recognize that the Church is called to be inclusive, yet never at the expense of Christian truth. Herein lies the dilemma facing all who are genuinely committed to the ecumenical journey.

In the figure of John Henry Newman, who is to be beatified on Sunday, we celebrate a churchman whose ecclesial vision was nurtured by his Anglican background and matured during his many years of ordained ministry in the Church of England. He can teach us the virtues that ecumenism demands: on the one hand, he was moved to follow his conscience, even at great personal cost; and on the other hand, the warmth of his continued friendship with his former colleagues, led him to explore with them, in a truly eirenical spirit, the questions on which they differed, driven by a deep longing for unity in faith. Your Grace, in that same spirit of friendship, let us renew our determination to pursue the goal of unity in faith, hope, and love, in accordance with the will of our one Lord and Saviour Jesus Christ.

With these sentiments, I take my leave of you. May the grace of the Lord Jesus Christ and the love of God and the fellowship of the Holy Spirit be with you all (2 Cor 13:13).

Joint Communiqué of Pope Benedict and the Archbishop of Canterbury

Shortly after their meeting at Lambeth Palace, this joint statement was issued.

Fifty years after the first meeting of a Pope and an Archbishop of Canterbury in modern times – that of Pope John XXIII and Archbishop Geoffrey Fisher, in December 1960 – Pope Benedict XVI paid a fraternal visit to Archbishop Rowan Williams.

In the first part of their meeting they both addressed the Anglican and Roman Catholic Diocesan Bishops of England, Scotland and Wales, in the Great Hall of the Archbishop's Library, before moving to a private meeting.

In the course of their private conversation, they addressed many of the issues of mutual concern to Anglicans and Roman Catholics. They affirmed the need to proclaim the Gospel message of salvation in Jesus Christ, both in a reasoned and convincing way in the contemporary context of profound cultural and social transformation, and in lives of holiness and transparency to God. They agreed on the importance of improving ecumenical relations and continuing theological dialogue in the face of new challenges to unity from within the Christian community and beyond it.

The Holy Father and the Archbishop reaffirmed the importance of continuing theological dialogue on the notion of the Church as communion, local and universal, and the implications of this concept for the discernment of ethical teaching.

They reflected together on the serious and difficult situation of Christians in the Middle East, and called upon all Christians to pray for their brothers and sisters and support their continued peaceful witness in the Holy Land. In the light of their recent public interventions, they also discussed the need to promote a courageous and generous engagement in the field of justice and peace, especially the needs of the poor, urging international leadership to fight hunger and disease.

Following their meeting they travelled together to the Palace of Westminster and to Evening Prayer at Westminster Abbey.

Westminster Hall, Palace of Westminster

Address to Politicians, Diplomats, Academics and Business Leaders

After his meeting with the Archbishop of Canterbury, the Pope travelled in the popemobile from Lambeth Palace across Lambeth Bridge and along Millbank to the Palace of Westminster. When he entered Westminster Hall to address leaders of civil society he paused at the spot at which Saint Thomas More, the Lord Chancellor of England, was tried and condemned to death in 1535 for refusing to acknowledge the King as also the head of the church. Among those gathered to hear the Pope's address were four former British Prime Ministers: Margaret Thatcher, John Major, Tony Blair and Gordon Brown.

Mr Speaker,

Thank you for your words of welcome on behalf of this distinguished gathering. As I address you, I am conscious of the privilege afforded me to speak to the British people and their representatives in Westminster Hall, a building of unique significance in the civil and political history of the people of these islands. Allow me also to express my esteem for the Parliament which has existed on this site for centuries and which has had such a profound influence on the development of participative government among the nations, especially in the

Commonwealth and the English-speaking world at large. Your common law tradition serves as the basis of legal systems in many parts of the world, and your particular vision of the respective rights and duties of the state and the individual, and of the separation of powers, remains an inspiration to many across the globe.

As I speak to you in this historic setting, I think of the countless men and women down the centuries who have played their part in the momentous events that have taken place within these walls and have shaped the lives of many generations of Britons, and others besides. In particular, I recall the figure of Saint Thomas More, the great English scholar and statesman, who is admired by believers and non-believers alike for the integrity with which he followed his conscience, even at the cost of displeasing the sovereign whose "good servant" he was, because he chose to serve God first. The dilemma which faced More in those difficult times, the perennial question of the relationship between what is owed to Caesar and what is owed to God, allows me the opportunity to reflect with you briefly on the proper place of religious belief within the political process.

This country's Parliamentary tradition owes much to the national instinct for moderation, to the desire to achieve a genuine balance between the legitimate claims of government and the rights of those subject to it. While decisive steps have been taken at several points in your history to place limits on the exercise of power, the nation's political institutions have been able to evolve with a remarkable degree of stability. In the process, Britain has emerged as a pluralist democracy which places great value on freedom of speech, freedom of political affiliation and respect for the rule of law, with a strong sense of the individual's rights and duties, and of the equality of all citizens before the law. While couched in different language, Catholic social teaching has much in common with this approach, in its overriding concern to safeguard the unique dignity of every human person, created in the image and likeness of God, and in its emphasis on the duty of civil authority to foster the common good.

And yet the fundamental questions at stake in Thomas More's trial continue to present themselves in ever-changing terms as new social conditions emerge. Each generation, as it seeks to advance the common good, must ask anew: what are the requirements that governments may reasonably impose upon citizens, and how far do they extend? By appeal to what authority can moral dilemmas be resolved? These questions take us directly to the ethical foundations of civil discourse. If the moral principles underpinning the democratic process are themselves determined by nothing more solid than social consensus, then the fragility of the process becomes all too evident – herein lies the real challenge for democracy.

The inadequacy of pragmatic, short-term solutions to complex social and ethical problems has been illustrated all too clearly by the recent global financial crisis. There is widespread agreement that the lack of a solid ethical foundation for economic activity has contributed to the grave difficulties now being experienced by millions of people throughout the world. Just as "every economic decision has a moral consequence" (*Caritas in Veritate*, 37), so too in the political field, the ethical dimension of policy has far-reaching consequences that no government can afford to ignore. A positive illustration of this is found in one of the British Parliament's particularly notable achievements – the abolition of the slave trade. The campaign that led to this landmark legislation was built upon firm ethical principles, rooted in the natural law, and it has made a contribution to civilization of which this nation may be justly proud.

The central question at issue, then, is this: where is the ethical foundation for political choices to be found? The Catholic tradition maintains that the objective norms governing right action are accessible to reason, prescinding from the content of revelation. According to this understanding, the role of religion in political debate is not so much to supply these norms, as if they could not be known by non-believers – still less to propose concrete political solutions, which would lie altogether outside the competence of religion – but rather to help purify and shed light upon the application of reason to the discovery of objective moral principles. This "corrective" role of religion vis-à-vis reason is not always welcomed, though, partly because distorted forms of religion, such as sectarianism and fundamentalism, can be seen to create serious social problems themselves. And in their turn, these distortions of religion arise when insufficient attention is given to the purifying and structuring role of reason within religion. It is a two-way process. Without the corrective supplied by religion, though, reason too can fall prey to distortions, as when it is manipulated by ideology, or applied in a partial way that fails to take full account of the dignity of the human person. Such misuse of reason, after all, was what gave rise to the slave trade in the first place and to many other social evils, not least the totalitarian ideologies of the twentieth century. This is why I would suggest that the world of reason and the world of faith – the world of secular rationality and the world of religious belief – need one another and should not be afraid to enter into a profound and ongoing dialogue, for the good of our civilization.

Religion, in other words, is not a problem for legislators to solve, but a vital contributor to the national conversation. In this light, I cannot but voice my concern at the increasing marginalization of religion, particularly of Christianity, that is taking place in some quarters, even in nations which place a great emphasis on tolerance. There are those who would advocate that the voice of religion be silenced, or at least relegated to the purely private sphere. There are those who argue that the public celebration of festivals such as Christmas should be discouraged, in the questionable belief that it might somehow offend those of other religions or none. And there are those who argue – paradoxically with the intention of eliminating discrimination – that Christians in public roles should be required at times to act against their conscience. These are worrying signs of a failure to appreciate not only the rights of believers to freedom of conscience and freedom of religion, but also the legitimate role of religion in the public square. I would invite all of you, therefore, within your respective spheres of influence, to seek ways of promoting and encouraging dialogue between faith and reason at every level of national life.

Your readiness to do so is already implied in the unprecedented invitation extended to me today. And it finds expression in the fields of concern in which your Government has been engaged with the Holy See. In the area of peace, there have been exchanges regarding the elaboration of an international arms trade treaty; regarding human rights, the Holy See and the United Kingdom have welcomed the spread of democracy, especially in the last sixty-five years; in the field of development, there has been collaboration on debt relief, fair trade and financing for development, particularly through the International Finance Facility, the International Immunization Bond, and the Advanced Market Commitment. The Holy See also looks forward to exploring with the United Kingdom new ways to promote environmental responsibility, to the benefit of all.

I also note that the present Government has committed the United Kingdom to devoting 0.7% of national income to development aid by 2013. In recent years it has been encouraging to witness the positive signs of a worldwide growth in solidarity towards the poor. But to turn this solidarity into effective action calls for fresh thinking that will improve life conditions in many important areas, such as food production, clean water, job creation, education, support to families, especially migrants, and basic healthcare. Where human lives are concerned, time is always short: yet the world has witnessed the vast resources that governments can draw upon to rescue financial institutions deemed "too big to fail". Surely the integral human development of the world's peoples is no less important: here is an enterprise, worthy of the world's attention, that is truly "too big to fail".

This overview of recent cooperation between the United Kingdom and the Holy See illustrates well how much progress has been made, in the years that have passed since the establishment of bilateral diplomatic relations, in promoting throughout the world the many core values that we share. I hope and pray that this relationship will continue to bear fruit, and that it will be mirrored in a growing acceptance of the need for dialogue and respect at every level of society between the world of reason and the world of faith. I am convinced that, within this country too, there are many areas in which the Church and the public authorities can work together for the good of citizens, in harmony with this Parliament's historic practice of invoking the Spirit's guidance upon those who seek to improve the conditions of all mankind. For such cooperation to be possible, religious bodies – including institutions linked to the Catholic Church – need to be free to act in accordance with their own principles and specific convictions based upon the faith and the official teaching of the Church. In this way, such basic rights as religious freedom, freedom of conscience and freedom of association are guaranteed. The angels looking down on us from the magnificent ceiling of this ancient Hall remind us of the long tradition from which British Parliamentary democracy has evolved. They remind us that God is constantly watching over us to guide and protect us. And they summon us to acknowledge the vital contribution that religious belief has made and can continue to make to the life of the nation.

Mr Speaker, I thank you once again for this opportunity briefly to address this distinguished audience. Let me assure you and the Lord Speaker of my continued good wishes and prayers for you and for the fruitful work of both Houses of this ancient Parliament. Thank you and God bless you all!

Westminster Abbey

Celebration of Evening Prayer: Introductory Words

From Westminster Hall Pope Benedict made the short journey to Westminster Abbey with the Archbishop of Canterbury to join other church leaders in a Service of Evening Prayer. The Archbishop of Canterbury welcomed him to the Abbey with the following words:

Your Holiness, brothers and sisters in Christ,

On behalf of the Christian communities of Britain, we welcome you in fraternal love to this great shrine, which has been of such significance for both Church and nation. For many centuries, the Daily Office of the Church has been celebrated here – first by Benedictine monks, then by the new foundation of the sixteenth century, always with the same rhythms of psalmody and petition, and the same purpose of glorifying God in all things.

As we join now in that unbroken tradition, we pray that our *sacrificium laudis*—our sacrifice of praise—will become more and more a sign of the sacrificial love which we offer together in Christ's name for the renewal of our society and our whole world in the power of his Spirit. May your visit be a blessing for all who share with you in pilgrimage and discipleship.

Pope Benedict responded as follows:

Your Grace, Mr Dean, Dear Friends in Christ,

I thank you for your gracious welcome. This noble edifice evokes England's long history, so deeply marked by the preaching of the Gospel and the Christian culture to which it gave birth. I come here today as a pilgrim from Rome, to pray before the tomb of Saint Edward the Confessor and to join you in imploring the gift of Christian unity. May these moments of prayer and friendship confirm us in love for Jesus Christ, our Lord and Saviour, and in common witness to the enduring power of the Gospel to illumine the future of this great nation.

Westminster Abbey

Address at a Service of Evening Prayer

From Westminster Hall Pope Benedict made the short journey to Westminster Abbey to join the Archbishop of Canterbury and other Church leaders in a Service of Evening Prayer. His visit began with a prayer for peace at the tomb of the Unknown Soldier. After venerating the sixth-century Canterbury Gospels, which had been brought to the Abbey from Corpus Christi College, Cambridge, the Pope and the Archbishop of Canterbury each gave an Address, before the two church leaders prayed together at the Shrine of St Edward the Confessor. The Pope spoke as follows:

Dear friends in Christ,

I thank the Lord for this opportunity to join you, the representatives of the Christian confessions present in Great Britain, in this magnificent Abbey Church dedicated to Saint Peter, whose architecture and history speak so eloquently of our common heritage of faith. Here we cannot help but be reminded of how greatly the Christian faith shaped the unity and culture of Europe and the heart and spirit of the English people. Here too, we are forcibly reminded that what we share, in Christ, is greater than what continues to divide us.

I am grateful to His Grace the Archbishop of Canterbury for his kind greeting, and to the Dean and Chapter of this venerable Abbey for their cordial welcome. I thank the Lord for allowing me, as the Successor of Saint Peter in the See of Rome, to make this pilgrimage to the tomb of Saint Edward the Confessor. Edward, King of England, remains a model of Christian witness and an example of that true grandeur to which the Lord summons his disciples in the Scriptures we have just heard: the grandeur of a humility and obedience grounded in Christ's own example (cf. Phil 2:6–8), the grandeur of a fidelity which does not hesitate to embrace the mystery of the Cross out of undying love for the divine Master and unfailing hope in his promises (cf. Mk 10:43–44).

This year, as we know, marks the hundredth anniversary of the modern ecumenical movement, which began with the Edinburgh Conference's appeal for Christian unity as the prerequisite for a credible and convincing witness to the Gospel in our time. In commemorating this anniversary, we must give thanks for the remarkable progress made towards this noble goal through the efforts of committed Christians of every denomination. At the same time, however, we remain conscious of how much yet remains to be done. In a world marked by growing interdependence and solidarity, we are challenged to proclaim with renewed conviction the reality of our reconciliation and liberation in Christ, and to propose the truth of the Gospel as the key to an authentic and integral human development. In a society which has become increasingly indifferent or even hostile to the Christian message, we are all the more compelled to give a joyful and convincing account of the hope that is within us (cf. 1 Pet 3:15), and to present the Risen Lord as the response to the deepest questions and spiritual aspirations of the men and women of our time.

As we processed to the chancel at the beginning of this service, the choir sang that Christ is our "sure foundation". He is the Eternal Son of God, of one substance with the Father, who took flesh, as the Creed states, "for us men and for our salvation". He alone has the words of everlasting life. In him, as the Apostle teaches, "all things hold together" … "for in him all the fullness of God was pleased to dwell" (Col 1:17,19).

Our commitment to Christian unity is born of nothing less than our faith in Christ, in this Christ, risen from the dead and seated at the right hand of the Father, who will come again in glory to judge the living and the dead. It is the reality of Christ's person, his saving work and above all the historical fact of his resurrection, which is the content of the apostolic *kerygma* and those credal formulas which, beginning in the New Testament itself, have guaranteed the integrity of its transmission. The Church's unity, in a word, can never be other than a unity in the apostolic faith, in the faith entrusted to each new member of the Body of Christ during the rite of Baptism. It is this faith which unites us to the Lord, makes us sharers in his Holy Spirit, and thus, even now, sharers in the life of the Blessed Trinity, the model of the Church's koinonia here below.

Dear friends, we are all aware of the challenges, the blessings, the disappointments and the signs of hope which have marked our ecumenical journey. Tonight we entrust all of these to the Lord, confident in his providence and the power of his grace. We know that the friendships we have forged, the dialogue which we have begun and the hope which guides us will provide strength and direction as we persevere on our common journey. At the same time, with evangelical realism, we must also recognize the challenges which confront us, not only along the path of Christian unity, but also in our task of proclaiming Christ in our day. Fidelity to the word of God, precisely because it is a true word, demands of us an obedience which leads us together to a deeper understanding of the Lord's will, an obedience which must be free of intellectual conformism or facile accommodation to the spirit of the age. This is the word of encouragement which I wish to leave with you this evening, and I do so in fidelity to my ministry as the Bishop of Rome and the Successor of Saint Peter, charged with a particular care for the unity of Christ's flock.

Gathered in this ancient monastic church, we can recall the example of a great Englishman and churchman whom we honour in common: Saint Bede the Venerable. At the dawn of a new age in the life of society and of the Church, Bede understood both the importance of fidelity to the word of God as transmitted by the apostolic tradition, and the need for creative openness to new developments and to the demands of a sound implantation of the Gospel in contemporary language and culture.

This nation, and the Europe which Bede and his contemporaries helped to build, once again stands at the threshold of a new age. May Saint Bede's example inspire the Christians of these lands to rediscover their shared legacy, to strengthen what they have in common, and to continue their efforts to grow in friendship. May the Risen Lord strengthen our efforts to mend the ruptures of the past and to meet the challenges of the present with hope in the future which, in his providence, he holds out to us and to our world. Amen.

Archbishop of Canterbury's address at Evening Prayer

Your Holiness,
Members of the Collegiate Body,
distinguished guests, brothers and sisters in Christ:

Christians in Britain, especially in England, look back with the most fervent gratitude to the events of 597, when Augustine landed on these shores to preach the gospel to the Anglo-Saxons at the behest of Pope Saint Gregory the Great. For Christians of all traditions and confessions, Saint Gregory is a figure of compelling attractiveness and spiritual authority – pastor and leader, scholar and exegete and spiritual guide. The fact that the first preaching of the Gospel to the English peoples in the sixth and seventh centuries has its origins in his vision creates a special connection for us with the See of the Apostles Peter and Paul; and Gregory's witness and legacy remain an immensely fruitful source of inspiration for our own mission in these dramatically different times. Two dimensions of that vision may be of special importance as we reflect today on the significance of Your Holiness's visit to us.

Saint Gregory was the first to spell out for the faithful something of the magnitude of the gift given to Christ's Church through the life of Saint Benedict – to whom you, Your Holiness, have signalled your devotion in the choice of your name as Pope. In Saint Gregory's Dialogues, we can trace the impact of Saint Benedict – an extraordinary man who, through a relatively brief Rule of life, opened up for the whole civilisation of Europe since the sixth century the possibility of living in joy and mutual service, in simplicity and self-denial, in a balanced pattern of labour and prayer in which every moment spoke of human dignity fully realised in surrender to a loving God. The Benedictine life proved a sure foundation not only for generations of monks and nuns, but for an entire culture in which productive work and contemplative silence and receptivity—human dignity and human freedom—were both honoured.

Our own culture, a culture in which so often it seems that "love has grown cold", is one in which we can see the dehumanising effects of losing sight of Benedict's vision. Work is so often an anxious and obsessive matter, as if our whole value as human beings depended upon it; and so, consequently, unemployment, still a scourge and a threat in these uncertain financial times, comes to seem like a loss of dignity and meaning in life. We live in an age where there is a desperate need to recover the sense of the dignity of both labour and leisure and the necessity of a silent openness to God that allows our true character to grow and flourish by participating in an eternal love.

In a series of profound and eloquent encyclicals, you have explored these themes for our day, grounding everything in the eternal love of the Holy Trinity, challenging us to hope both for this world and the next, and analysing the ways in which our economic habits have trapped us in a reductive and unworthy style of human living. In this building with its long Benedictine legacy, we acknowledge with gratitude your contribution to a Benedictine vision for our days, and pray that your time with us in Britain may help us all towards a renewal of the hope and energy we need as Christians to witness to our conviction that in their relation to God men and women may grow into the fullest freedom and beauty of spirit.

And in this, we are recalled also to the importance among the titles of the Bishops of Rome of St Gregory's own self-designation as "servant of the servants of God" – surely the one title that points most directly to the example of the Lord who has called us. There is, we know, no authority in the Church that is not the authority of service: that is, of building up the people of God to full maturity. Christ's service is simply the way in which we meet his almighty power: the power to remake the world he has created, pouring out into our lives, individually and together, what we truly need in order to become fully what we are made to be – the image of the divine life. It is that image which the pastor in the Church seeks to serve, bowing down in reverence before each human person in the knowledge of the glory for which he or she was made.

Christians have very diverse views about the nature of the vocation that belongs to the See of Rome. Yet, as Your Holiness's great predecessor reminded us all in his encyclical *Ut Unum Sint*, we must learn to reflect together on how the historic ministry of the Roman Church and its chief pastor may speak to the Church catholic—East and West, global north and global south of the authority of Christ and his apostles to build up the Body in love; how it may be realized as a ministry of patience and reverence towards all, a ministry of creative love and self-giving that leads us all into the same path of seeking not our own comfort or profit but the good of the entire human community and the glory of God the creator and redeemer.

We pray that your time with us will be a further step for all of us into the mystery of the cross and the resurrection, so that growing together we may become more effective channels for God's purpose to heal the wounds of humankind, and to restore once again both in our societies and our environment the likeness of his glory as revealed in the face of Jesus Christ.

Saturday
18 September

Westminster Cathedral

Homily at Mass at Westminster Cathedral

On Saturday morning, at Archbishop's House, Westminster, Pope Benedict received courtesy calls from the Prime Minister, David Cameron, the Deputy Prime Minister, Nick Clegg, and the Acting Leader of the Opposition, Harriet Harman. He then presided at a celebration of Mass in Cathedral of the Most Precious Blood of Our Lord Jesus Christ, Westminster. He delivered this homily.

Dear Friends in Christ,

I greet all of you with joy in the Lord and I thank you for your warm reception. I am grateful to Archbishop Nichols for his words of welcome on your behalf. Truly, in this meeting of the Successor of Peter and the faithful of Britain, "heart speaks unto heart" as we rejoice in the love of Christ and in our common profession of the Catholic faith which comes to us from the Apostles. I am especially happy that our meeting takes place in this

Cathedral dedicated to the Most Precious Blood, which is the sign of God's redemptive mercy poured out upon the world through the passion, death and resurrection of his Son, our Lord Jesus Christ. In a particular way I greet the Archbishop of Canterbury, who honours us by his presence.

The visitor to this Cathedral cannot fail to be struck by the great crucifix dominating the nave, which portrays Christ's body, crushed by suffering, overwhelmed by sorrow, the innocent victim whose death has reconciled us with the Father and given us a share in the very life of God. The Lord's outstretched arms seem to embrace this entire church, lifting up to the Father all the ranks of the faithful who gather around the altar of the Eucharistic sacrifice and share in its fruits. The crucified Lord stands above and before us as the source of our life and salvation, "the high priest of the good things to come", as the author of the Letter to the Hebrews calls him in today's first reading (Heb 9:11).

It is in the shadow, so to speak, of this striking image, that I would like to consider the word of God which has been proclaimed in our midst and reflect on the mystery of the Precious Blood. For that mystery leads us to see the unity between Christ's sacrifice on the Cross, the Eucharistic sacrifice which he has given to his Church, and his eternal priesthood, whereby, seated at the right hand of the Father, he makes unceasing intercession for us, the members of his mystical body.

Let us begin with the sacrifice of the Cross. The outpouring of Christ's blood is the source of the Church's life. Saint John, as we know, sees in the water and blood which flowed from our Lord's body the wellspring of that divine life which is bestowed by the Holy Spirit and communicated to us in the sacraments (Jn 19:34; cf. 1 Jn1:7; 5:6–7). The Letter to the Hebrews draws out, we might say, the liturgical implications of this mystery. Jesus, by his suffering and death, his self-oblation in the eternal Spirit, has become our high priest and "the mediator of a new covenant" (Heb 9:15). These words echo our Lord's own words at the Last Supper, when he instituted the Eucharist as the sacrament of his body, given up for us, and his blood, the blood of the new and everlasting covenant shed for the forgiveness of sins (cf. Mk 14:24; Mt 26:28; Lk 22:20).

Faithful to Christ's command to "do this in memory of me" (Lk 22:19), the Church in every time and place celebrates the Eucharist until the Lord returns in glory, rejoicing in his sacramental presence and drawing upon the power of his saving sacrifice for the redemption of the world. The reality of the Eucharistic sacrifice has always been at the heart of Catholic faith; called into question in the sixteenth century, it was solemnly reaffirmed at the Council of Trent against the backdrop of our justification in Christ. Here in England, as we know, there were many who staunchly defended the

Mass, often at great cost, giving rise to that devotion to the Most Holy Eucharist which has been a hallmark of Catholicism in these lands.

The Eucharistic sacrifice of the Body and Blood of Christ embraces in turn the mystery of our Lord's continuing passion in the members of his Mystical Body, the Church in every age. Here the great crucifix which towers above us serves as a reminder that Christ, our eternal high priest, daily unites our own sacrifices, our own sufferings, our own needs, hopes and aspirations, to the infinite merits of his sacrifice. Through him, with him, and in him, we lift up our own bodies as a sacrifice holy and acceptable to God (cf. Rom 12:1). In this sense we are caught up in his eternal oblation, completing, as Saint Paul says, in our flesh what is lacking in Christ's afflictions for the sake of his body, the Church (cf. Col 1:24). In the life of the Church, in her trials and tribulations, Christ continues, in the stark phrase of Pascal, to be in agony until the end of the world (*Pensées*, 553, éd. Brunschvicg).

We see this aspect of the mystery of Christ's precious blood represented, most eloquently, by the martyrs of every age, who drank from the cup which Christ himself drank, and whose own blood, shed in union with his sacrifice, gives new life to the Church. It is also reflected in our brothers and sisters throughout the world who even now are suffering discrimination and persecution for their Christian faith. Yet it is also present, often hidden in the suffering of all those individual Christians who daily unite their sacrifices to those of the Lord for the sanctification of the Church and the redemption of the world. My thoughts go in a special way to all those who are spiritually united with this Eucharistic celebration, and in particular the sick, the elderly, the handicapped and those who suffer mentally and spiritually.

Here too I think of the immense suffering caused by the abuse of children, especially within the Church and by her ministers. Above all, I express my deep sorrow to the innocent victims of these unspeakable crimes, along with my hope that the power of Christ's grace, his sacrifice of reconciliation, will bring deep healing and peace to their lives. I also acknowledge, with you, the shame and humiliation which all of us have suffered because of these sins; and I invite you to offer it to the Lord with trust that this chastisement will contribute to the healing of the victims, the purification of the Church and the renewal of her age-old commitment to the education and care of young people. I express my gratitude for the efforts being made to address this problem responsibly, and I ask all of you to show your concern for the victims and solidarity with your priests.

Dear friends, let us return to the contemplation of the great crucifix which rises above us. Our Lord's hands, extended on the Cross, also invite us to contemplate our participation in his eternal priesthood and thus our responsibility, as members of his body, to bring the reconciling power of his sacrifice to the world in which we live. The Second Vatican Council spoke eloquently of the indispensable role of the laity in carrying forward the Church's mission through their efforts to serve as a leaven of the Gospel in society and to work for the advancement of God's Kingdom in the world (cf. *Lumen Gentium*, 31; *Apostolicam Actuositatem*, 7). The Council's appeal to the lay faithful to take up their baptismal sharing in Christ's mission echoed the insights and teachings of John Henry Newman. May the profound ideas of this great Englishman continue to inspire all Christ's followers in this land to conform their every thought, word and action to Christ, and to work strenuously to defend those unchanging moral truths which, taken up, illuminated and confirmed by the Gospel, stand at the foundation of a truly humane, just and free society.

How much contemporary society needs this witness! How much we need, in the Church and in society, witnesses of the beauty of holiness, witnesses of the splendour of truth, witnesses of the joy and freedom born of a living relationship with Christ! One of the greatest challenges facing us today is how to speak convincingly of the wisdom and liberating power of God's word to a world which all too often sees the Gospel as a constriction of human freedom, instead of the truth which liberates our minds and enlightens our efforts to live wisely and well, both as individuals and as members of society.

Let us pray, then, that the Catholics of this land will become ever more conscious of their dignity as a priestly people, called to consecrate the world to God through lives of faith and holiness. And may this increase of apostolic zeal be accompanied by an outpouring of prayer for vocations to the ordained priesthood. For the more the lay apostolate grows, the more urgently the need for priests is felt; and the more the laity's own sense of vocation is deepened, the more what is proper to the priest stands out. May many young men in this land find the strength to answer the Master's call to the ministerial priesthood, devoting their lives, their energy and their talents to God, thus building up his people in unity and fidelity to the Gospel, especially through the celebration of the Eucharistic sacrifice.

Dear friends, in this Cathedral of the Most Precious Blood, I invite you once more to look to Christ, who leads us in our faith and brings it to perfection (cf.Heb 12:2). I ask you to unite yourselves ever more fully to the Lord, sharing in his sacrifice on the Cross and offering him that "spiritual worship" (Rom 12:1) which embraces every aspect of our lives and finds expression in our efforts to contribute to the coming of his Kingdom. I pray that, in doing so, you may join the ranks of faithful believers throughout the long Christian history of this land in building a society truly worthy of man, worthy of your nation's highest traditions.

Piazza, Westminster Cathedral

Message to Young People

After Mass, Pope Benedict greeted 2,500 young people who had gathered in the Piazza.

Dear young friends, thank you for your warm welcome.

"Heart Speaks unto heart." As you know I chose these words so dear to Cardinal Newman as the theme of my visit. In these few moments that we are together I wish to speak to you from my own heart, and I ask to open your hearts to what I have to say.

I ask each of you first and foremost to look into your own heart, think of all the love that your heart was made to receive, and also love it is meant to give, after all we were made for love. This is what the Bible means when it says that we are made in the image and likeness of God. We were made to know the God of love, the God who is father, son and Holy Spirit, and to find our supreme fulfilment in that Divine love that knows no beginning or end.

We were made to receive love, and we have. Every day we should thank God for the love we have already known. For the love that has made us who we are. The love that is shown us what is truly important in life. We need to thank the Lord for the love we have received from our families, our friends, our teachers, and all those people in our lives who have helped us to realise how precious we are in their eyes, and in the eyes of God.

We were also made to give love, to make the inspirational for all we do, and the most enduring thing in our lives. At times it seems so natural, especially when we feel the exhilaration of love, when our hearts brim over with generosity, idealism, the desire to help others to build a better world – but at other times, we realise it is difficult to love. Our hearts can easily be hardened by selfishness, envy and pride. The Blessed Mother Teresa of Calcutta, the great missionary of charity reminded us that giving love, pure and generous love, is the fruit of a daily decision.

Every day we have to choose to love and this requires help. The help that comes from Christ, from the wisdom found in his word. And from the Grace which he bestows us in the sacraments of his church. This is the message I want to share with you today. I ask you to look into your hearts, each day, to find the source of all true love. Jesus is always there. Quietly waiting for us to be still with him and to hear his voice. Deep within your heart, he is calling you to spend time with him in prayer, but this kind of prayer, real prayer, requires discipline.

It requires time for moments of silence every day. Often it means waiting for the Lord to speak.

Even amidst the business and stress of our daily lives we need to make space for silence, because it is in silence that we find God. And in silence that we discover our true self.

And in discovering our true self we discover the particular vocation which God has given us for the building up of his church and the redemption of our world. Heart speaks unto heart. With these words from my heart, dear young friends, I assure you of my prayers for you.

That our lives will bear fruit of the cross, of the civilisation of the cross, I ask you to pray for me, for my Ministry as the successor of Peter, and for the needs of the church throughout the world. Upon you, your families and friends, I call on you God's blessing of wisdom, joy and peace.

Westminster Cathedral, Chapel of St Paul

Message to the Faithful of Wales

After his meeting with young people, Pope Benedict blessed a mosaic of Saint David in the cathedral, and greeted the people of Wales with the following words.

Dear Bishop Regan,

Thank you for your very warm greeting on behalf of the faithful of Wales. I am happy to have this opportunity to honour the nation and its ancient Christian traditions by blessing a mosaic of Saint David, the patron saint of the Welsh people, and by lighting the candle of the statue of Our Lady of Cardigan.

Saint David was one of the great saints of the sixth century, that golden age of saints and missionaries in these isles, and he was thus a founder of the Christian culture which lies at the root of modern Europe. David's preaching was simple yet profound: his dying words to his monks were, "Be joyful, keep the faith, and do the little things". It is the little things that reveal our love for the one who loved us first (cf. *1* Jn 4:19) and that bind people into a community of faith, love and service. May Saint David's message, in all its simplicity and richness, continue to resound in Wales today, drawing the hearts of its people to renewed love for Christ and his Church.

Through the ages the Welsh people have been distinguished for their devotion to the Mother of God; this is evidenced by the innumerable places in Wales called "Llanfair" – Mary's Church. As I prepare to light the candle held by Our Lady, I pray that she will continue to intercede with her Son for all the men and women of Wales. May the light of Christ continue to guide their steps and shape the life and culture of the nation.

Sadly, it was not possible for me to come to Wales during this visit. But I trust that this beautiful statue, which now returns to the National Shrine of Our Lady in Cardigan, will be a lasting reminder of the Pope's deep love for the Welsh people, and of his constant closeness, both in prayer and in the communion of the Church.

Bendith Duw ar bobol Cymru! God bless the people of Wales!

Apostolic Nunciature, Wimbledon

Meeting with people sexually abused by Catholic priests

On Saturday afternoon, the Pope held a private meeting at the Apostolic Nunciature with a group of people who have been sexually abused by members of the clergy. Afterwards, the following statement describing what happened was released:

He [the Pope] was moved by what they had to say and expressed his deep sorrow and shame over what victims and their families had suffered. He prayed with them and assured them that the Catholic Church is continuing to implement effective measures designed to safeguard young people, and that it is doing all in its power to investigate allegations, to collaborate with civil authorities and to bring to justice clergy and religious accused of these egregious crimes.

As he has done on other occasions, he prayed that all the victims of abuse might experience healing and reconciliation, and be able to overcome their past and present distress with serenity and hope for the future.

St Peter's Residence, Lambeth

Address to those responsible for child protection

Following the private meeting at the home of the Apostolic Nuncio, the Holy Father addressed a group of professionals and volunteers dedicated to the safeguarding of children and young people in Catholic parishes and schools.

Dear Friends,

I am glad to have the opportunity to greet you, who represent the many professionals and volunteers responsible for child protection in church environments. The Church has a long tradition of caring for children from their earliest years through to adulthood, following the affectionate example of Christ, who blessed the children brought to him, and who taught his disciples that to such as these the Kingdom of Heaven belongs (cf. Mk 10:13–16).

Your work, carried out within the framework of the recommendations made in the first instance by the Nolan Report and subsequently by the Cumberlege Commission, has made a vital contribution to the promotion of safe environments for young people. It helps to ensure that the preventative measures put in place are effective, that they are maintained with vigilance, and that any allegations of abuse are dealt with swiftly and justly. On behalf of the many children you serve and their parents, let me thank you for the good work that you have done and continue to do in this field.

It is deplorable that, in such marked contrast to the Church's long tradition of care for them, children have suffered abuse and mistreatment at the hands of some priests and religious. We have all become much more aware of the need to safeguard children, and you are an important part of the Church's broad-ranging response to the problem. While there are never grounds for complacency, credit should be given where it is due: the efforts of the Church in this country and elsewhere, especially in the last ten years, to guarantee the safety of children and young people and to show them every respect as they grow to maturity, should be acknowledged. I pray that your generous service will help to reinforce an atmosphere of trust and renewed commitment to the welfare of children, who are such a precious gift from God.

May God prosper your work, and may he pour out his blessings upon all of you.

St Peter's Residence, Lambeth

Speech to St Peter's Residents and Staff

The Pope then visited the elderly residents of St Peter's Residence, the care home run by the Little Sisters of the Poor. He was welcomed by Sr Marie Claire, who spoke of St Jeanne Jugan, the founder of the Little Sisters. The Pope replied as follows.

My dear Brothers and Sisters,

I am very pleased to be among you, the residents of Saint Peter's, and to thank Sister Marie Claire and Mrs Fasky for their kind words of welcome on your behalf. I am also pleased to greet Archbishop Smith of Southwark, as well as the Little Sisters of the Poor and the personnel and volunteers who look after you.

As advances in medicine and other factors lead to increased longevity, it is important to recognize the presence of growing numbers of older people as a blessing for society. Every generation can learn from the experience and wisdom of the generation that preceded it. Indeed the provision of care for the elderly should be considered not so much an act of generosity as the repayment of a debt of gratitude.

For her part, the Church has always had great respect for the elderly. The Fourth Commandment, "Honour your father and your mother as the Lord your God commanded you" (Deut 5:16), is linked to the promise, "that your days may be prolonged, and that it may go well with you, in the land which the Lord your God gives you" (Deut 5:16). This work of the Church for the aging and infirm not only provides love and care for them, but is also rewarded by God with the blessings he promises on the land where this commandment is observed. God wills a proper respect for the dignity and worth, the health and well-being of the elderly and, through her charitable institutions in Britain and beyond, the Church seeks to fulfil the Lord's command to respect life, regardless of age or circumstances.

At the very start of my pontificate I said, "Each of us is willed, each of us is loved, each of us is necessary" (Homily at the Mass for the Beginning of the Petrine Ministry of the Bishop of Rome, 24 April 2005). Life is a unique gift, at every stage from conception until natural death, and it is God's alone to give and to take. One may enjoy good health in old age; but equally Christians should not be afraid to share in the suffering of Christ, if God wills that we struggle with infirmity. My predecessor, the late Pope John Paul, suffered very publicly during the last years of his life. It was clear to all of us that he did so in union with the sufferings of our Saviour. His cheerfulness and forbearance as he faced his final days were a remarkable and moving example to all of us who have to carry the burden of advancing years.

In this sense, I come among you not only as a father, but also as a brother who knows well the joys and the struggles that come with age. Our long years of life afford us the opportunity to appreciate both the beauty of God's greatest gift to us, the gift of life, as well as the fragility of the human spirit. Those of us who live many years are given a marvellous chance to deepen our awareness of the mystery of Christ, who humbled himself to share in our humanity. As the normal span of our lives increases, our physical capacities are often diminished; and yet these times may well be among the most spiritually fruitful years of our lives. These years are an opportunity to remember in affectionate prayer all those whom we have cherished in this life, and to place all that we have personally been and done before the mercy and tenderness of God. This will surely be a great spiritual comfort and enable us to discover anew his love and goodness all the days of our life.

With these sentiments, dear brothers and sisters, I am pleased to assure you of my prayers for you all, and I ask for your prayers for me. May our blessed Lady and her spouse Saint Joseph intercede for our happiness in this life and obtain for us the blessing of a serene passage to the next.

May God bless you all!

Hyde Park

Homily at the Prayer Vigil

On Saturday evening, Pope Benedict travelled in the popemobile along Horse Guards Road, The Mall, Constitution Hill and Hyde Park Corner before arriving at Hyde Park, where more than 80,000 pilgrims had amassed to join him for a Vigil of Prayer, including the Rite of Eucharistic Exposition and Benediction. He spoke as follows.

My Brothers and Sisters in Christ,

This is an evening of joy, of immense spiritual joy, for all of us. We are gathered here in prayerful vigil to prepare for tomorrow's Mass, during which a great son of this nation, Cardinal John Henry Newman, will be declared Blessed. How many people, in England and throughout the world, have longed for this moment! It is also a great joy for me, personally, to share this experience with you. As you know, Newman has long been an important influence in my own life and thought, as he has been for so many people beyond these isles. The drama of Newman's life invites us to examine our lives, to see them against the vast horizon of God's plan, and to grow in communion with the Church of every time and place: the Church of the apostles, the Church of the martyrs, the Church of the saints, the Church which Newman loved and to whose mission he devoted his entire life.

I thank Archbishop Peter Smith for his kind words of welcome in your name, and I am especially pleased to see the many young people who are present for this vigil. This evening, in the context of our common prayer, I would like to reflect with you about a few aspects of Newman's life which I consider very relevant to our lives as believers and to the life of the Church today.

Let me begin by recalling that Newman, by his own account, traced the course of his whole life back to a powerful experience of conversion which he had as a young man. It was an immediate experience of the truth of God's word, of the objective reality of Christian revelation as handed down in the Church. This experience, at once religious and intellectual, would inspire his vocation to be a minister of the Gospel, his discernment of the source of authoritative teaching in the Church of God, and his zeal for the renewal of ecclesial life in fidelity to the apostolic tradition. At the end of his life, Newman would describe his life's work as a struggle against the growing tendency to view religion as a purely private and subjective matter, a question of personal opinion. Here is the first lesson we can learn from his life: in our day, when an intellectual and moral relativism threatens to sap the very foundations of our society, Newman reminds us that, as men and women made in the image and likeness of God, we were created to know the truth, to find in that truth our ultimate freedom and the fulfilment of our deepest human aspirations. In a word, we are meant to know Christ, who is himself "the way, and the truth, and the life" (Jn 14:6).

Newman's life also teaches us that passion for the truth, intellectual honesty and genuine conversion are costly. The truth that sets us free cannot be kept to ourselves; it calls for testimony, it begs to be heard, and in the end its convincing power comes from itself and not from the human eloquence or arguments in which it may be couched. Not far from here, at Tyburn, great numbers of our brothers and sisters died for the faith; the witness of their fidelity to the end was ever more powerful than the inspired words that so many of them spoke before surrendering everything to the Lord. In our own time, the price to be paid for fidelity to the Gospel is no longer being hanged, drawn and quartered but it often involves being dismissed out of hand, ridiculed or parodied. And yet, the Church cannot withdraw from the task of proclaiming Christ and his Gospel as saving truth, the source of our ultimate happiness as individuals and as the foundation of a just and humane society.

Finally, Newman teaches us that if we have accepted the truth of Christ and committed our lives to him, there can be no separation between what we believe and the way we live our lives. Our every thought, word and action must be directed to the glory of God and the spread of his Kingdom. Newman understood this, and was the great champion of the prophetic office of the Christian laity. He saw clearly that we do not so much accept the truth in a purely intellectual act as embrace it in a spiritual dynamic that penetrates to the core of our being. Truth is passed on not merely by formal teaching, important as that is, but also by the witness of lives lived in integrity, fidelity and holiness; those who live in and by the truth instinctively recognize what is false and, precisely as false, inimical to the beauty and goodness which accompany the splendour of truth, *veritatis splendor*.

Tonight's first reading is the magnificent prayer in which Saint Paul asks that we be granted to know "the love of Christ which surpasses all understanding" (Eph 3:14–21). The Apostle prays that Christ may dwell in our hearts through faith (cf. Eph 3:17) and that we may come to "grasp, with all the saints, the breadth and the length, the height and the depth" of that love. Through faith we come to see God's word as a lamp for our steps and light for our path (cf. Ps 119:105). Newman, like the countless saints who preceded him along the path of Christian discipleship, taught that the "kindly light" of faith leads us to realize the truth about ourselves, our dignity as God's children, and the sublime destiny which awaits us in heaven. By letting the light of faith shine in our hearts, and by abiding in that light through our daily union with the Lord in prayer and participation in the life-giving sacraments of the Church, we ourselves become light to those around us; we exercise our "prophetic office"; often, without even knowing it, we draw people one step closer to the Lord and his truth. Without the life of prayer, without the interior transformation which takes place through the grace of the sacraments, we cannot, in Newman's words, "radiate Christ"; we become just another "clashing cymbal" (1 Cor 13:1) in a world filled with growing noise and confusion, filled with false paths leading only to heartbreak and illusion.

One of the Cardinal's best-loved meditations includes the words, "God has created me to do him some definite service. He has committed some work to me which he has not committed to another" (*Meditations on Christian Doctrine*). Here we see Newman's fine Christian realism, the point at which faith and life inevitably intersect. Faith is meant to bear fruit in the transformation of our world through the power of the Holy Spirit at work in the lives and activity of believers. No one who looks realistically at our world today could think that Christians can afford to go on with business as usual, ignoring the profound crisis of faith which has overtaken our society, or simply trusting that the patrimony of values handed down by the Christian centuries will continue to inspire and shape the future of our society. We know that in times of crisis and upheaval God has raised up great saints and prophets for the renewal of the Church and Christian society; we trust in his providence and we pray for his continued guidance. But each of us, in accordance with his or her state of life, is called to work for the advancement of God's Kingdom by imbuing temporal life with the values of the Gospel. Each of us has a mission, each of us is called to change the world, to work for a culture of life, a culture forged by love and respect for the dignity of each human person. As our Lord tells us in the Gospel we have just heard, our light must shine in the sight of all, so that, seeing our good works, they may give praise to our heavenly Father (cf. Mt 5:16).

Here I wish to say a special word to the many young people present. Dear young friends: only Jesus knows what "definite service" he has in mind for you. Be open to his voice resounding in the depths of your heart: even now his heart is speaking to your heart. Christ has need of families to remind the world of the dignity of human love and the beauty of family life. He needs men and women who devote their lives to the noble task of education, tending the young and forming them in the ways of the Gospel. He needs those who will consecrate their lives to the pursuit of perfect charity, following him in chastity, poverty and obedience, and serving him in the least of our brothers and sisters. He needs the powerful love of contemplative religious, who sustain the Church's witness and activity through their constant prayer. And he needs priests, good and holy priests, men who are willing to lay down their lives for their sheep.

Ask our Lord what he has in mind for you! Ask him for the generosity to say "yes!" Do not be afraid to give yourself totally to Jesus. He will give you the grace you need to fulfil your vocation. Let me finish these few words by warmly inviting you to join me next year in Madrid for World Youth Day. It is always a wonderful occasion to grow in love for Christ and to be encouraged in a joyful life of faith along with thousands of other young people. I hope to see many of you there!

And now, dear friends, let us continue our vigil of prayer by preparing to encounter Christ, present among us in the Blessed Sacrament of the Altar. Together, in the silence of our common adoration, let us open our minds and hearts to his presence, his love, and the convincing power of his truth. In a special way, let us thank him for the enduring witness to that truth offered by Cardinal John Henry Newman. Trusting in his prayers, let us ask the Lord to illumine our path, and the path of all British society, with the kindly light of his truth, his love and his peace. Amen.

Sunday
19 September

Cofton Park, Birmingham

Beatification Homily

Hundreds of well-wishers turned out to wave Pope Benedict off as he left the Apostolic Nunciature in Wimbledon on Sunday morning to fly by helicopter to Birmingham. He presided at the Mass of Beatification of John Henry Newman at Cofton Park with a congregation estimated at 65,000. After the reading of the Gospel by Deacon Jack Sullivan, whose back cure had paved the way for the Beatification, the Pope preached the following homily.

Dear Brothers and Sisters in Christ,

This day that has brought us together here in Birmingham is a most auspicious one. In the first place, it is the Lord's day, Sunday, the day when our Lord Jesus Christ rose from the dead and changed the course of human history for ever, offering new life and hope to all who live in darkness and in the shadow of death. That is why Christians all over the world come together on this day to give praise and thanks to God for the great marvels he has worked for us. This particular Sunday also marks a significant moment in the life of the British nation, as it is the day chosen to commemorate the seventieth anniversary of the Battle of Britain. For me as one who lived and suffered through the dark days of the Nazi regime in Germany, it is deeply moving to be here with you on this occasion, and to recall how many of your fellow citizens sacrificed their lives, courageously resisting the forces of that evil ideology. My thoughts go in particular to nearby Coventry, which suffered such heavy bombardment and massive loss of life in November 1940. Seventy years later, we recall with shame and horror the dreadful toll of death and destruction that war brings in its wake, and we renew our resolve to work for peace and reconciliation wherever the threat of conflict looms. Yet there is another, more joyful reason why this is an auspicious day for Great Britain, for the Midlands, for Birmingham. It is the day that sees Cardinal John Henry Newman formally raised to the altars and declared Blessed.

I thank Archbishop Bernard Longley for his gracious welcome at the start of Mass this morning. I pay tribute to all who have worked so hard over many years to promote the cause of Cardinal Newman, including the Fathers of the Birmingham Oratory and the members of the Spiritual Family Das Werk. And I greet everyone here from Great Britain, Ireland, and further afield; I thank you for your presence at this celebration, in which we give glory and praise to God for the heroic virtue of a saintly Englishman.

England has a long tradition of martyr saints, whose courageous witness has sustained and inspired the Catholic community here for centuries. Yet it is right and fitting that we should recognize today the holiness of a confessor, a son of this nation who, while not called to shed his blood for the Lord, nevertheless bore eloquent witness to him in the course of a long life devoted to the priestly ministry, and especially to preaching, teaching, and writing. He is worthy to take his place in a long line of saints and scholars from these islands, Saint Bede, Saint Hilda, Saint Aelred, Blessed Duns Scotus, to name but a few. In Blessed John Henry, that tradition of gentle scholarship, deep human wisdom and profound love for the Lord has borne rich fruit, as a sign of the abiding presence of the Holy Spirit deep within the heart of God's people, bringing forth abundant gifts of holiness.

Cardinal Newman's motto, *Cor ad cor loquitur*, or "Heart speaks unto heart", gives us an insight into his understanding of the Christian life as a call to holiness, experienced as the profound desire of the human heart to enter into intimate communion with the Heart of God. He reminds us that faithfulness to prayer gradually transforms us into the divine likeness. As he wrote in one of his many fine sermons, "a habit of prayer, the practice of turning to God and the unseen world in every season, in every place, in every emergency – prayer, I say, has what may be called a natural effect in spiritualizing and elevating the soul. A man is no longer what he was before; gradually ... he has imbibed a new set of ideas, and become imbued with fresh principles" (*Parochial and Plain Sermons*, iv, 230–231). Today's Gospel tells us that no one can be the servant of two masters (cf. Lk 16:13), and Blessed John Henry's teaching on prayer explains how the faithful Christian is definitively taken into the service of the one true Master, who alone has a claim to our unconditional devotion (cf. Mt 23:10). Newman helps us to understand what this means for our daily lives: he tells us that our divine Master has assigned a specific task to each one of us, a "definite service", committed uniquely to every single person: "I have my mission", he wrote, "I am a link in a chain, a bond of connexion between persons. He has not created me for naught. I shall do good, I shall do his work; I shall be an angel of peace, a preacher of truth in my own place ... if I do but keep his commandments and serve him in my calling" (*Meditations and Devotions*, 301–2).

The definite service to which Blessed John Henry was called involved applying his keen intellect and his prolific pen to many of the most pressing "subjects of the day". His insights into the relationship between faith and reason, into the vital place of revealed religion in civilized society, and into the need for a broadly-based and wide-ranging approach to education were not only of profound importance for Victorian England, but continue today to inspire and enlighten many all over the world. I would like to pay particular tribute to his vision for education, which has done so much to shape the ethos that is the driving force behind Catholic schools and colleges today. Firmly opposed to any reductive or utilitarian approach, he sought to achieve an educational environment in which intellectual training, moral discipline and religious commitment would come together. The project to found a Catholic University in Ireland provided him with an opportunity to develop his ideas on the subject, and the collection of discourses that he published as *The Idea of a University* holds up an ideal from which all those engaged in academic formation can continue to learn. And indeed, what better goal could teachers of religion set themselves than Blessed John Henry's famous appeal for an intelligent, well-instructed laity: "I want a laity, not arrogant, not rash in speech, not disputatious, but men who know their religion, who enter into it, who know just where they stand, who know what they hold and what they do not, who know their creed so well that they can give an account of it, who know so much of history that they can defend it" (*The Present Position of Catholics in England*, ix, 390). On this day when the author of those words is raised to the altars, I pray that, through his intercession and example, all who are engaged in the task of teaching and catechesis will be inspired to greater effort by the vision he so clearly sets before us.

While it is John Henry Newman's intellectual legacy that has understandably received most attention in the vast literature devoted to his life and work, I prefer on this occasion to conclude with a brief reflection on his life as a priest, a pastor of souls. The warmth and humanity underlying his appreciation of the pastoral ministry is beautifully expressed in another of his famous sermons: "Had Angels been your priests, my brethren, they could not have condoled with you, sympathized with you, have had compassion on you, felt tenderly for you, and made allowances for you, as we can; they could not have been your patterns and guides, and have led you on from your old selves into a new life, as they can who come from the midst of you" ("Men, not Angels: the Priests of the Gospel", *Discourses to Mixed Congregations*, 3). He lived out that profoundly human vision of priestly ministry in his devoted care for the people of Birmingham during the years that he spent at the Oratory he founded, visiting the sick and the poor, comforting the bereaved, caring for those in prison. No wonder that on his death so many thousands of people lined the local streets as his body was taken to its place of burial not half a mile from here. One hundred and twenty years later, great crowds have assembled once again to rejoice in the Church's solemn recognition of the outstanding holiness of this much-loved father of souls. What better way to express the joy of this moment than by turning to our heavenly Father in heartfelt thanksgiving, praying in the words that Blessed John Henry Newman placed on the lips of the choirs of angels in heaven:

Praise to the Holiest in the height
And in the depth be praise;
In all his words most wonderful,
Most sure in all his ways!
(*The Dream of Gerontius*).

Cofton Park, Birmingham

Angelus Domini

At the conclusion of the Beatification Mass, Pope Benedict delivered his weekly Angelus address.

Brothers and Sisters in Jesus Christ,

I am pleased to send my greetings to the people of Seville where, just yesterday, Madre María de la Purísima de la Cruz was beatified. May Blessed María be an inspiration to young women to follow her example of single-minded love of God and neighbour.

When Blessed John Henry Newman came to live in Birmingham, he gave the name "Maryvale" to his first home here. The Oratory that he founded is dedicated to the Immaculate Conception of the Blessed Virgin. And the Catholic University of Ireland he placed under the patronage of Mary, *Sedes Sapientiae*. In so many ways, he lived his priestly ministry in a spirit of filial devotion to the Mother of God. Meditating upon her role in the unfolding of God's plan for our salvation, he was moved to exclaim: "Who can estimate the holiness and perfection of her, who was chosen to be the Mother of Christ? What must have been her gifts, who was chosen to be the only near earthly relative of the Son of God, the only one whom He was bound by nature to revere and look up to; the one appointed to train and educate Him, to instruct Him day by day, as He grew in wisdom and in stature?" (*Parochial and Plain Sermons*, ii, 131–2). It is on account of those abundant gifts of grace that we honour her, and it is on account of that intimacy with her divine Son that we naturally seek her intercession for our own needs and the needs of the whole world. In the words of the Angelus, we turn now to our Blessed Mother and commend to her the intentions that we hold in our hearts.

Oscott College

Address to the Bishops of England, Scotland and Wales

After the Beatification ceremonies, Pope Benedict made a private visit to the Oratory of Saint Philip Neri in Edgbas-

ton, where he toured Newman's rooms, before joining the bishops of England, Wales and Scotland for lunch at St Mary's College, Oscott, the Birmingham archdiocesan seminary. After addressing the bishops, the Pope met the seminarians of England, Wales and Scotland in the grounds of Oscott College before leaving for the farewell ceremony at Birmingham airport. This is his speech to the bishops:

My dear Brother Bishops,

This has been a day of great joy for the Catholic community in these islands. Blessed John Henry Newman, as we may now call him, has been raised to the altars as an example of heroic faithfulness to the Gospel and an intercessor for the Church in this land that he loved and served so well. Here in this very chapel in 1852, he gave voice to the new confidence and vitality of the Catholic community in England and Wales after the restoration of the hierarchy, and his words could be applied equally to Scotland a quarter of a century later. His beatification today is a reminder of the Holy Spirit's continuing action in calling forth gifts of holiness from among the people of Great Britain, so that from east to west and from north to south, a perfect offering of praise and thanksgiving may be made to the glory of God's name.

I thank Cardinal O'Brien and Archbishop Nichols for their words, and in so doing, I am reminded how recently I was able to welcome all of you to Rome for the Ad Limina visits of your respective Episcopal Conferences. We spoke then about some of the challenges you face as you lead your people in faith, particularly regarding the urgent need to proclaim the Gospel afresh in a highly secularized environment. In the course of my visit it has become clear to me how deep a thirst there is among the British people for the Good News of Jesus Christ. You have been chosen by God to offer them the living water of the Gospel, encouraging them to place their hopes, not in the vain enticements of this world, but in the firm assurances of the next. As you proclaim the coming of the Kingdom, with its promise of hope for the poor and the needy, the sick and the elderly, the unborn and the neglected, be sure to present in its fulness the life-giving message of the Gospel, including those elements which call into question the widespread assumptions of today's culture. As you know, a Pontifical Council has recently been established for the New Evangelization of countries of long-standing Christian tradition, and I would encourage you to avail yourselves of its services in addressing the task before you. Moreover, many of the new ecclesial movements have a particular charism for evangelization, and I know that you will continue to explore appropriate and effective ways of involving them in the mission of the Church.

Since your visit to Rome, political changes in the United Kingdom have focused attention on the consequences of the financial crisis, which has caused so much hardship to countless individuals and families. The spectre of unemployment is casting its shadow over many people's lives, and the long-term cost of the ill-advised investment practices of recent times is becoming all too evident. In these circumstances, there will be additional calls on the characteristic generosity of British Catholics, and I know that you will take a lead in calling for solidarity with those in need. The prophetic voice of Christians has an important role in highlighting the needs of the poor and disadvantaged, who can so easily be overlooked in the allocation of limited resources. In their teaching document *Choosing the Common Good*, the Bishops of England and Wales underlined the importance of the practice of virtue in public life. Today's circumstances provide a good opportunity to reinforce that message, and indeed to encourage people to aspire to higher moral values in every area of their lives, against a background of growing cynicism regarding even the possibility of virtuous living.

Another matter which has received much attention in recent months, and which seriously undermines the moral credibility of Church leaders, is the shameful abuse of children and young people by priests and religious. I have spoken on many occasions of the deep wounds that such behaviour causes, in the victims first and foremost, but also in the relationships of trust that should exist between priests and people, between priests and their bishops, and between the Church authorities and the public. I know that you have taken serious steps to remedy this situation, to ensure that children are effectively protected from harm and to deal properly and transparently with allegations as they arise. You have publicly acknowledged your deep regret over what has happened, and the often inadequate ways it was addressed in the past. Your growing awareness of the extent of child abuse in society, its devastating effects, and the need to provide proper victim support should serve as an incentive to share the lessons you have learned with the wider community. Indeed, what better way could there be of making reparation for these sins than by reaching out, in a humble spirit of compassion, towards children who continue to suffer abuse elsewhere? Our duty of care towards the young demands nothing less.

As we reflect on the human frailty that these tragic events so starkly reveal, we are reminded that, if we are to be effective Christian leaders, we must live lives of the utmost integrity, humility and holiness. As Blessed John Henry Newman once wrote, "O that God would grant the clergy to feel their weakness as sinful men, and the people to sympathize with them and love them and pray for their increase in all good gifts of grace" (Sermon, 22 March 1829). I pray that among the graces of this visit will be a renewed dedication on the part of Christian leaders to the prophetic vocation they have received, and a new appreciation on the part of the people for the great gift of the ordained ministry. Prayer for vocations will then arise spontaneously, and we may be confident that the Lord will respond by sending labourers to bring in the plentiful harvest that he has prepared throughout the United Kingdom (cf. Mt 9:37–38). In this regard, I am glad that I will shortly have the opportunity to meet the seminarians of England, Scotland and Wales, and to assure them of my prayers as they prepare to play their part in bringing in that harvest.

Finally, I should like to speak to you about two specific matters that affect your episcopal ministry at this time. One is the imminent publication of the new translation of the Roman Missal. I want to take this opportunity to thank all of you for the contribution you have made, with such painstaking care, to the collegial exercise of reviewing and approving the texts. This has provided an immense service to Catholics throughout the English-speaking world. I encourage you now to seize the opportunity that the new translation offers for in-depth catechesis on the Eucharist and renewed devotion in the manner of its celebration. "The more lively the eucharistic faith of the people of God, the deeper is its sharing in ecclesial life in steadfast commitment to the mission entrusted by Christ to his disciples" (*Sacramentum Caritatis*, 6). The other matter I touched upon in February with the Bishops of England and Wales, when I asked you to be generous in implementing the Apostolic Constitution *Anglicanorum Coetibus.* This should be seen as a prophetic gesture that can contribute positively to the developing relations between Anglicans and Catholics. It helps us to set our sights on the ultimate goal of all ecumenical activity: the restoration of full ecclesial communion in the context of which the mutual exchange of gifts from our respective spiritual patrimonies serves as an enrichment to us all. Let us continue to pray and work unceasingly in order to hasten the joyful day when that goal can be accomplished.

With these sentiments, I thank you warmly for your hospitality over the past four days. Commending all of you and the people you serve to the intercession of Saint Andrew, Saint David and Saint George, I am pleased to impart my Apostolic Blessing to you and to all the clergy, religious and lay faithful of England, Scotland and Wales.

Birmingham International Airport

Farewell Address

At the State Farewell Ceremony at Birmingham airport, the Prime Minister, David Cameron, wished the Pope and his delegation a safe return to Rome. "This brings to a close an incredibly moving four days for our country", the Prime Minister said. "Faith is part of the fabric of our country. It always has been and it always will be. As you, your Holiness, have said, faith is not a problem for legislators to solve but rather a vital part of our national conversation. And we are proud of that. But people do not have to share a religious faith or agree with religion on everything to see the benefit of asking the searching questions that you, your Holiness, have posed to us about our society and how we treat ourselves and each other. You have really challenged the whole country to sit up and think, and that can only be a good thing." Pope Benedict responded as follows:

Prime Minister,

Thank you for your kind words of farewell on behalf of Her Majesty's Government and the people of the United Kingdom. I am very grateful for all the hard work of preparation, on the part of both the present and the previous Government, the civil service, local authorities and police, and the many volunteers who patiently helped to prepare for the events of these four days. Thank you for the warmth of your welcome and for the hospitality that I have enjoyed.

During my time with you, I have been able to meet representatives of the many communities, cultures, languages and religions that make up British society. The very diversity of modern Britain is a challenge to its

Government and people, but it also represents a great opportunity to further intercultural and interreligious dialogue for the enrichment of the entire community.

In these days, I was grateful for the opportunity to meet Her Majesty The Queen, as well as yourself and other political leaders, and to be able to discuss matters of common interest, both at home and abroad. I was particularly honoured to be invited to address both Houses of Parliament in the historic precincts of Westminster Hall. I sincerely hope that these occasions will contribute to confirming and strengthening the excellent relations between the Holy See and the United Kingdom, especially in cooperation for international development, in care for the natural environment, and in the building of a civil society with a renewed sense of shared values and common purpose.

It was also my pleasure to visit His Grace the Archbishop of Canterbury and the Bishops of the Church of England, and later to pray with them and our fellow Christians in the evocative surroundings of Westminster Abbey, a place which speaks so eloquently of our shared traditions and culture. As Britain is home to so many religious traditions, I was grateful to have the opportunity to meet their representatives and to share some thoughts with them about the contribution that the religions can offer to the development of a healthy pluralistic society.

Naturally, my visit was directed in a special way to the Catholics of the United Kingdom. I treasure the time spent with the bishops, clergy, religious and laity, and with teachers, pupils and older people. It was especially moving to celebrate with them, here in Birmingham, the beatification of a great son of England, Cardinal John Henry Newman. With his vast legacy of scholarly and spiritual writings, I am certain that he still has much to teach us about Christian living and witness amid the challenges of today's world, challenges which he foresaw with such remarkable clarity.

As I take my leave of you, let me assure you once again of my good wishes and prayers for the peace and prosperity of Great Britain. Thank you very much and God bless you all!